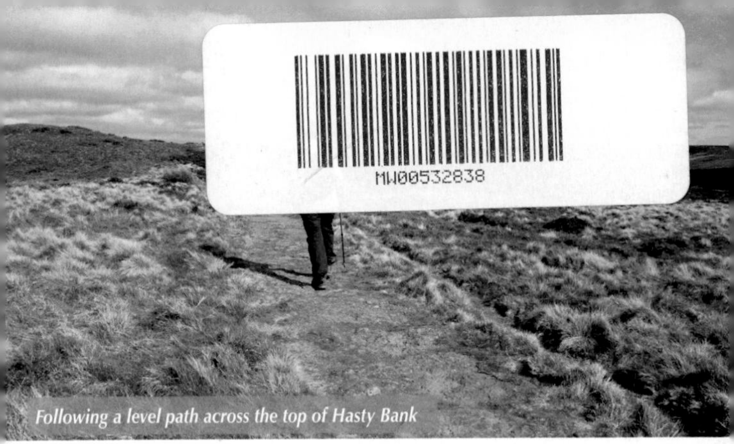

Following a level path across the top of Hasty Bank

THE CLEVELAND WAY NATIONAL TRAIL

Officially opened in 1969, the Cleveland Way was the second national trail to be established in Britain. Stretching 110 miles (177km) from Helmsley to Filey, it takes in open heather moorlands, gentle dales and dramatic cliff coastline. The trail is suitable for walkers and trekkers at all levels of experience.

Contents and using this guide

This booklet of Ordnance Survey 1:25,000 Explorer maps has been designed for convenient use on the trail and includes:

- a key to map pages (page 2) showing where to find the maps for each stage
- the full and up-to-date line of the National Trail
- an extract from the OS Explorer map legend (pages 56–58)

In addition, the guidebook *Walking the Cleveland Way and Yorkshire Wolds Way* describes the full route with lots of other practical and historical information.

ISBN-13: 978 1 85284 934 4

Map data

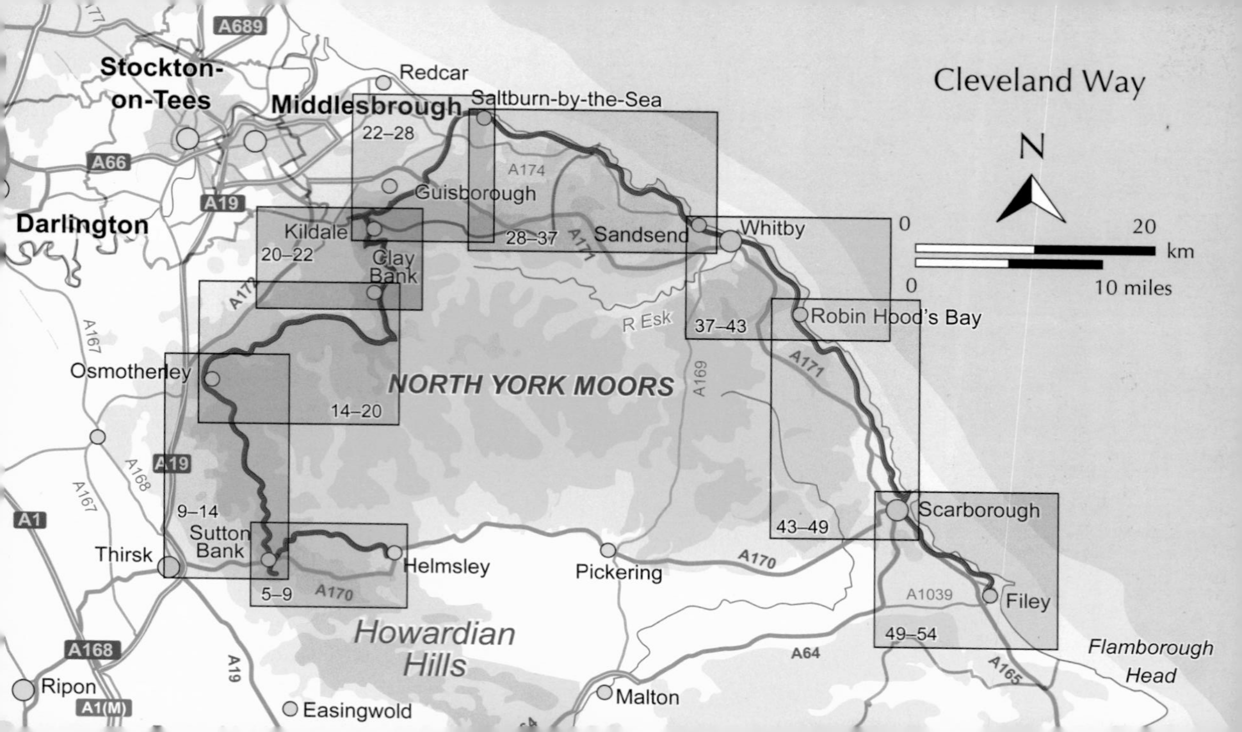
Cleveland Way
N
0
20
km
0
10 miles
Stockton-on-Tees
Middlesbrough
Redcar
Saltburn-by-the-Sea
Darlington
Guisborough
Kildale
Clay Bank
Sandsend
Whitby
Robin Hood's Bay
Scarborough
Filey
Flamborough Head
Osmotherley
NORTH YORK MOORS
R Esk
Sutton Bank
Thirsk
Helmsley
Pickering
Malton
Howardian Hills
Easingwold
Ripon
22–28
28–37
20–22
37–43
14–20
43–49
9–14
5–9
49–54
A689
A66
A19
A174
A171
A172
A169
A167
A168
A170
A1039
A64
A165
A1
A1(M)

THE CLEVELAND WAY NATIONAL TRAIL

Route symbols on OS map extracts

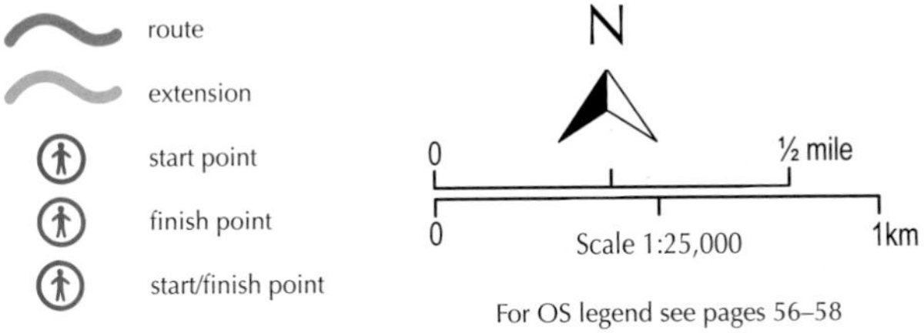

For OS legend see pages 56–58

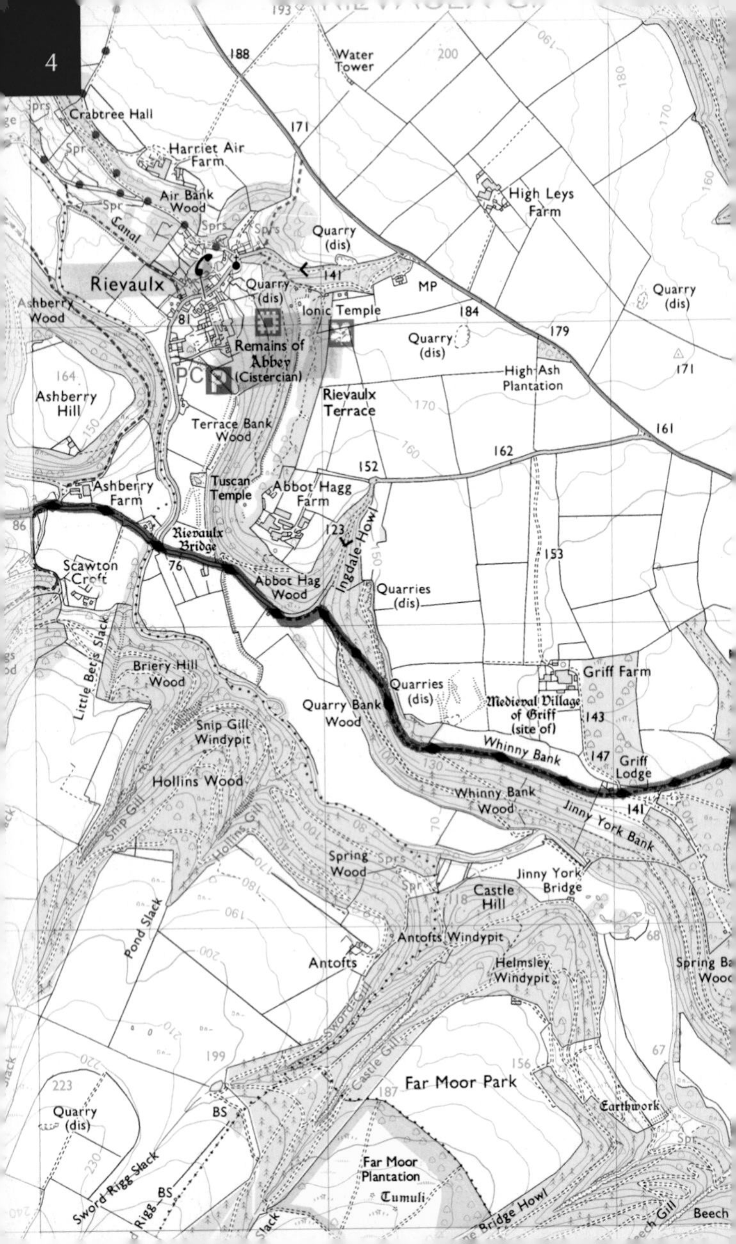
Crabtree Hall
Harriet Air Farm
Air Bank Wood
Canal
Rievaulx
Ashberry Wood
Ashberry Hill
Water Tower
Quarry (dis)
Remains of Abbey (Cistercian)
Ionic Temple
High Leys Farm
Quarry (dis)
MP
High Ash Plantation
Rievaulx Terrace
Terrace Bank Wood
Tuscan Temple
Abbot Hagg Farm
Ashberry Farm
Rievaulx Bridge
Scawton Croft
Abbot Hag Wood
Ingdale Howl
Quarries (dis)
Little Bet's Slack
Briery Hill Wood
Quarry Bank Wood
Griff Farm
Medieval Village of Griff (site of)
Whinny Bank
Griff Lodge
Snip Gill Windypit
Hollins Wood
Whinny Bank Wood
Jinny York Bank
Snip Gill
Hollins Gill
Spring Wood
Jinny York Bridge
Castle Hill
Pond Slack
Antofts Windypit
Antofts
Helmsley Windypit
Spring Bank Wood
Sword Gill
Castle Gill
Far Moor Park
Earthwork
Quarry (dis)
Sword Rigg Slack
Far Moor Plantation
Tumuli
Bridge Howl
Beech Gill
Beech

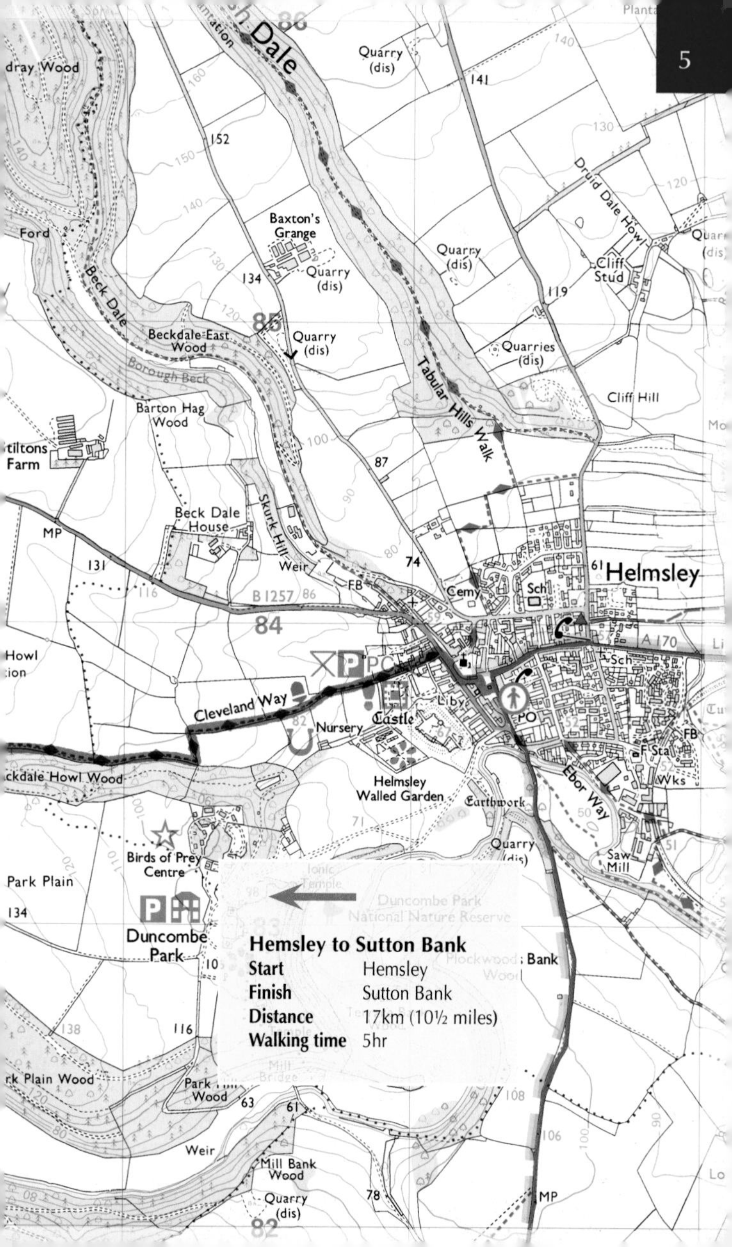

Hemsley to Sutton Bank

Start	Hemsley
Finish	Sutton Bank
Distance	17km (10½ miles)
Walking time	5hr

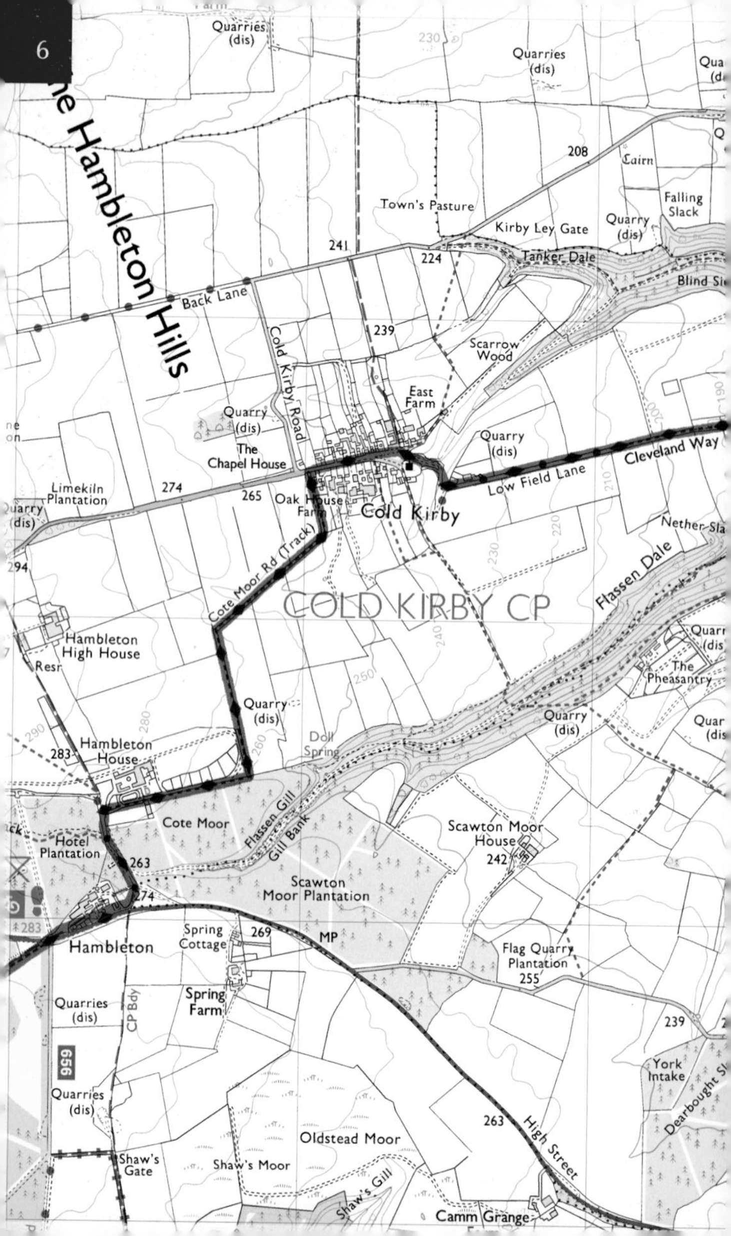

Quarries (dis)
230
Quarries (dis)
208
Cairn
Falling Slack
Town's Pasture
Kirby Ley Gate
Quarry (dis)
241
224
Tanker Dale
Blind Si
Back Lane
The Hambleton Hills
Cold Kirby Road
239
Scarrow Wood
East Farm
Quarry (dis)
The Chapel House
Quarry (dis)
Cleveland Way
Low Field Lane
Limekiln Plantation
274
265
Oak House Farm
Cold Kirby
Nether Sla
294
Cote Moor Rd (Track)
COLD KIRBY CP
Flassen Dale
Hambleton High House
Resr
Quarry (dis)
The Pheasantry
250
240
230
220
210
200
190
Quarry (dis)
Doll Spring
290
280
260
Hambleton House
283
Cote Moor
Flassen Gill
Gill Bank
Hotel Plantation
263
274
Scawton Moor House
242
Scawton Moor Plantation
283
Hambleton
Spring Cottage
269
MP
Flag Quarry Plantation
255
Quarries (dis)
CP Bdy
Spring Farm
239
York Intake
Dearbought Sl
Quarries (dis)
263
High Street
Oldstead Moor
Shaw's Gate
Shaw's Moor
Shaw's Gill
Camm Grange

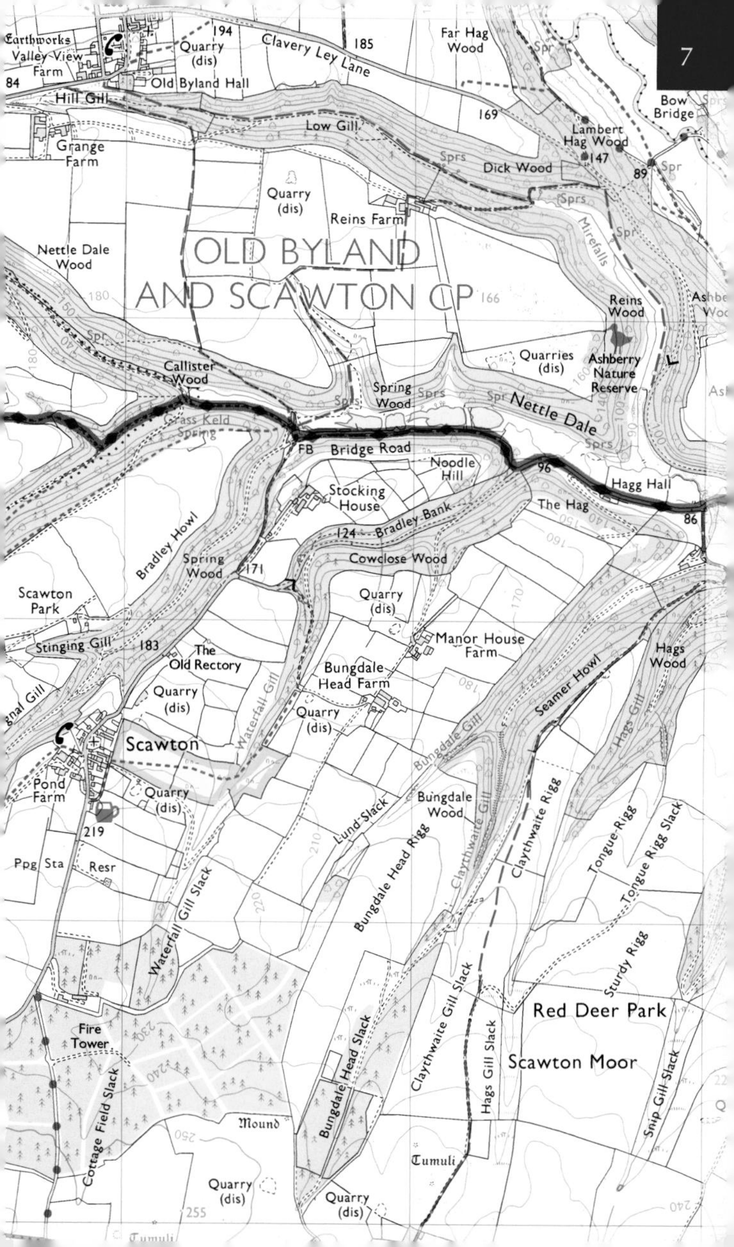
Earthworks
Valley View Farm
84
194
Quarry (dis)
Old Byland Hall
Clavery Ley Lane
185
Far Hag Wood
Spr
Bow Bridge
Hill Gill
Low Gill
169
Lambert Hag Wood
147
89
Grange Farm
Sprs
Dick Wood
Quarry (dis)
Reins Farm
Mirefalls
Nettle Dale Wood
OLD BYLAND AND SCAWTON CP
180
166
150
140
Reins Wood
Ashberry Nature Reserve
Quarries (dis)
Callister Wood
Spring Wood
Nettle Dale
Grass Keld Spring
FB
Bridge Road
Noodle Hill
96
Hagg Hall
86
Stocking House
The Hag
Bradley Howl
124
Bradley Bank
Cowclose Wood
Spring Wood
171
Scawton Park
Quarry (dis)
Manor House Farm
Stinging Gill
183
The Old Rectory
Bungdale Head Farm
Hags Wood
Seamer Howl
Quarry (dis)
Quarry (dis)
Waterfall Gill
Bungdale Gill
Hags Gill
Scawton
Pond Farm
Quarry (dis)
Bungdale Wood
219
Lund Slack
Claythwaite Gill
Claythwaite Rigg
Tongue Rigg
Tongue Rigg Slack
Ppg Sta
Resr
Waterfall Gill Slack
Bungdale Head Rigg
210
220
Sturdy Rigg
Fire Tower
Claythwaite Gill Slack
Red Deer Park
Bungdale Head Slack
Hags Gill Slack
Scawton Moor
Cottage Field Slack
230
240
250
Mound
Snip Gill Slack
Tumuli
Quarry (dis)
Quarry (dis)
255
Tumuli

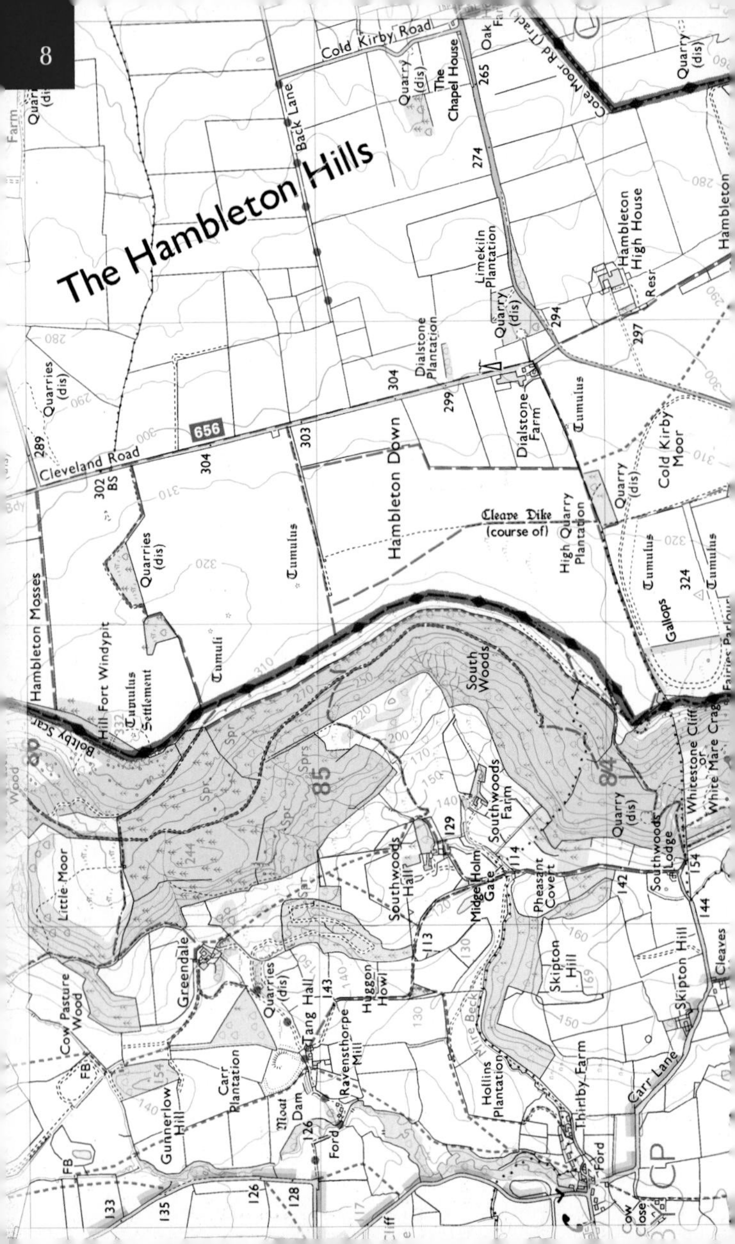
The Hambleton Hills
Cold Kirby Road
Back Lane
The Chapel House
Quarry (dis)
Oak Farm
Cote Moor Rd (Track)
Limekiln Plantation
Hambleton High House
Resr
Hambleton
Dialstone Plantation
Dialstone Farm
Tumulus
Cold Kirby Moor
Cleveland Road
656
Hambleton Down
Cleave Dike (course of)
High Quarry Plantation
Gallops
Fairies Parlour
Quarries (dis)
Hambleton Mosses
Hill Fort Windypit
Tumulus
Settlement
Tumuli
Boltby Scar
South Woods
Southwoods Farm
Southwoods Hall
Whitestone Cliff or White Mare Crag
Southwoods Lodge
Little Moor
Greendale
Cow Pasture Wood
Tang Hall
Huggon Howl
Midge Holm Gate
Pheasant Covert
Skipton Hill
Cleaves
Ravensthorpe Mill
Carr Plantation
Gunnerlow Hill
Moat
Dam
Ford
Hollins Plantation
Thirlby Farm
Carr Lane
Cow Close
Wood
FB
Bdy
BS
Spr
Sprs
85
84
80

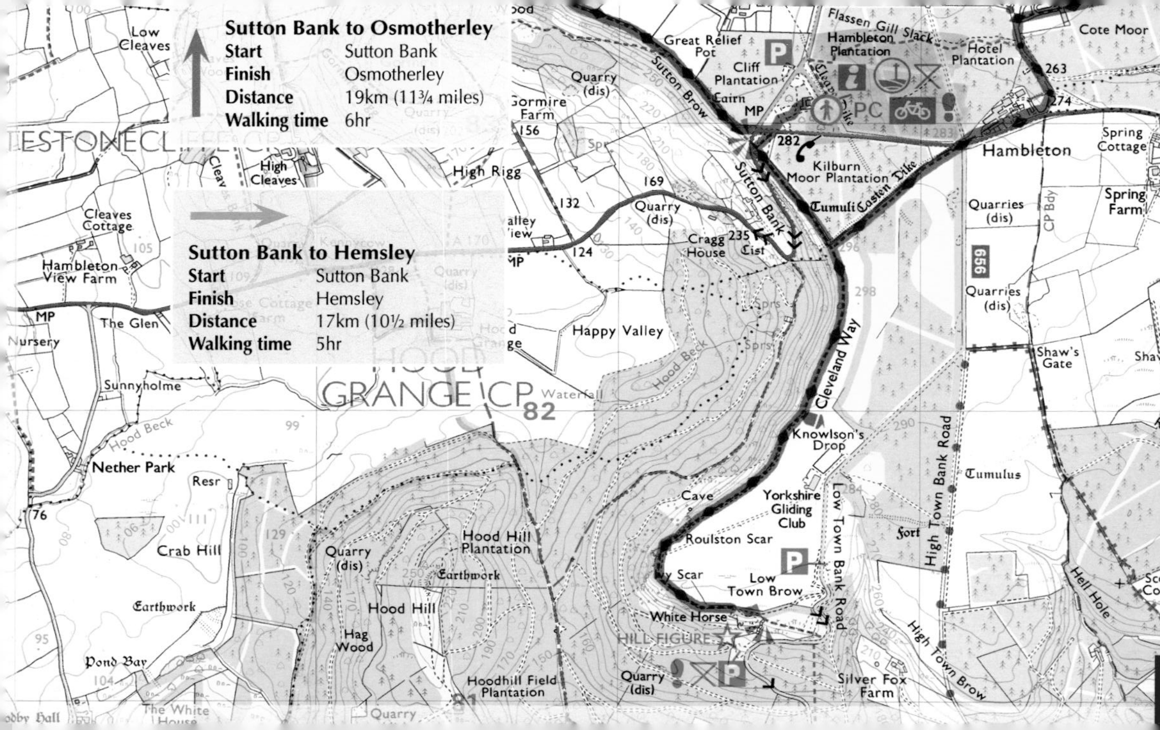
Sutton Bank to Osmotherley
Start Sutton Bank
Finish Osmotherley
Distance 19km (11¾ miles)
Walking time 6hr
Sutton Bank to Hemsley
Start Sutton Bank
Finish Hemsley
Distance 17km (10½ miles)
Walking time 5hr
Low Cleaves
High Cleaves
Cleaves Cottage
Hambleton View Farm
The Glen
Nursery
Sunnyholme
Hood Beck
Nether Park
Resr
Crab Hill
Earthwork
Pond Bay
The White House
HOOD GRANGE CP
82
Waterfall
Happy Valley
High Rigg
Gormire Farm
Quarry (dis)
Great Relief Pot
Cliff Plantation
Cairn
MP
Sutton Brow
Sutton Bank
Cragg House
Cist
Kilburn Moor Plantation
Tumuli
Casten Dike
Hambleton Plantation
Flassen Gill Slack
Hotel Plantation
Cote Moor
Flassen Gill
Gill Bank
Hambleton
Spring Cottage
Spring Farm
Quarries (dis)
CP Bdy
656
Shaw's Gate
Shaw's Moor
Cleveland Way
Knowlson's Drop
Yorkshire Gliding Club
Cave
Roulston Scar
Low Town Brow
Low Town Bank Road
High Town Bank Road
High Town Brow
Tumulus
Fort
Ravens Gill
High Wood
Hell Hole
Scotch Corner
White Horse
HILL FIGURE
Silver Fox Farm
Hood Hill Plantation
Hood Hill
Hag Wood
Hoodhill Field Plantation

Thorodale Wood
Ford
Arden Bank
Stoney Gill Hole
North Wood
Quarry (dis)
Quarries (dis)
Gowerdale Windypits
Earthwork
Dale Town Common
Hambleton Road
Murton Common
High Paradise
Little Moor
Steeple Cross (BS)
CP Bdy
Long Barrow
Tumuli
Clarke Scars
New Plantation
Gallow Hill
Silver Nab
Cracoe
Cracoe Slack
Windy Gill
North Woods
Northwoods Slack
Newfound England
Resr
Windygill Ridge
Haggitt Hill
Ridge End
Tumulus (rems of)
Boltby Moor
Boltby Forest

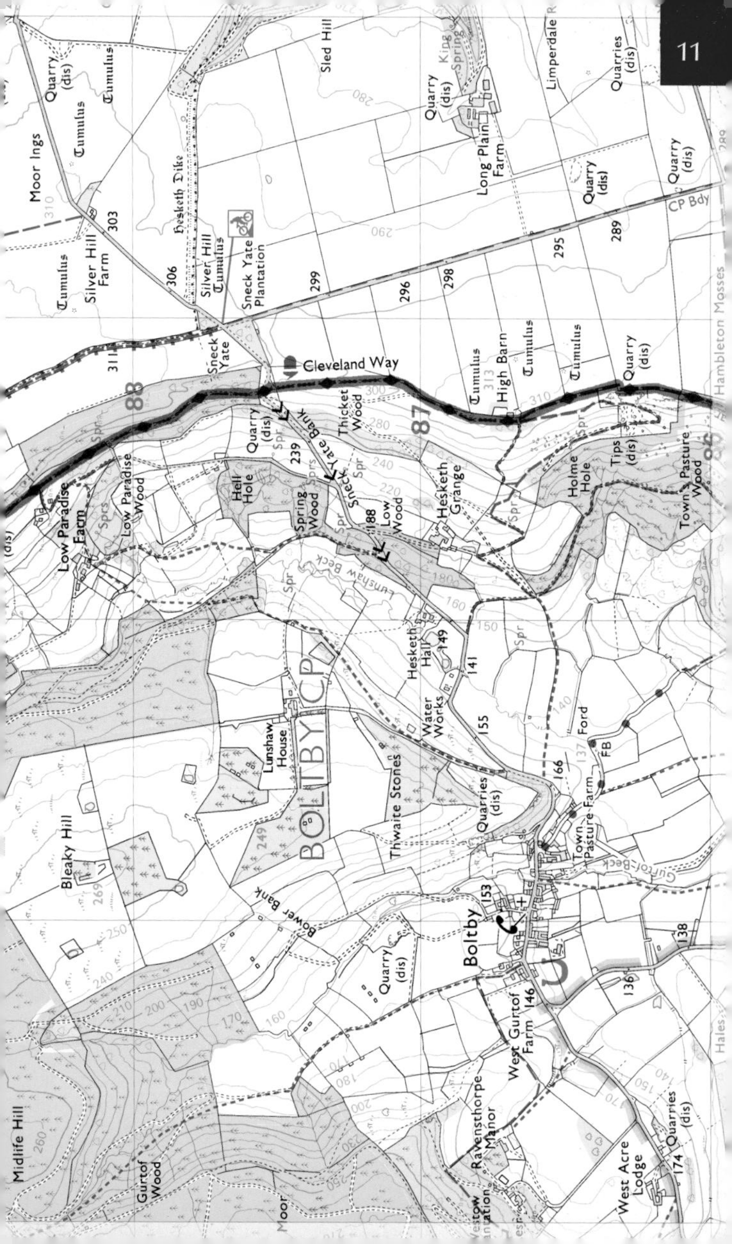

Moor Ings
Quarry (dis)
Tumulus
Silver Hill Farm
303
306
Hesketh Dike
Silver Hill Tumulus
Sneck Yate Plantation
Sled Hill
King's Spring
Quarry (dis)
Long Plain Farm
Limperdale R
Quarries (dis)
Quarry (dis)
CP Bdy
299
296
298
295
289
Sneck Yate
311
88
Cleveland Way
Quarry (dis)
239
Sneck Yate Bank
Thicket Wood
87
Tumulus
313
High Barn
Hambleton Mosses
Low Paradise Farm
Low Paradise Wood
Sprs
Spr
Hell Hole
Spring Wood
188
Low Wood
Hesketh Grange
Holme Hole
Tips (dis)
Town's Pasture Wood
Lunshaw Beck
Hesketh Hall
149
141
150
160
Water Works
155
Lunshaw House
BOLTBY CP
Thwaite Stones
Quarries (dis)
Ford
FB
166
137
140
Town Pasture Farm
Gurtof Beck
Bleaky Hill
269
249
Bower Bank
153
Boltby
Quarry (dis)
146
West Gurtof Farm
136
138
Midlife Hill
260
Gurtof Wood
Moor
Ravensthorpe Manor
West Acre Lodge
174
Quarries (dis)
Hales

Square Corner
Thimbleby Moor
The Intake
Nine Stones
High Grain Moor
Over Silton Moor
Mother Dale
Crabtree Bank Plantation
Moor Ridge
Mother Gill
Black Hill
Hambleton End
399
Black Hambleton
Tumulus
Cleveland Way
CP Bdy
Dodd End
Pie Shaw Corner
Pie Shaw
Swinestone Cliff
Nether Silton Moor
Burton's Plantation
Robinson's Cross (remains of)
Bawderis Intake
Bawderis Wood
Bawderis Beck
Locker Low Moor
Locker Bank
Dale Head
Cringle Ing Slack
Whitestones
656
65
286
279
261
186

Wild Middle
Ford
Sprs
Spr
Grouse Butts
White Gill Head
BS
Whitestones
Cairns
372
384
(Track)
Quarries (disused)
Quarries (disused)
Quarries (disused)
Quarries (disused)
358
Tumulus
Tumulus
Tumulus
Quarry (dis)
365
350
370
380
360
330
Whitestone Scar
Kepwick Moor
289
Sheepfold
White Gill
Quarry (disused)
Marl Pits
Dunsforth's Hill
Kepwick Quarry (disused)
Tumuli
Old Gill
Warren Wood
Quarry (dis)
Waind's Intake Plantation
247
194
FB
FBs
Quarry
KEPWICK CP
Nab Hill
Nab Farm
Pit (dis)
French Hill Wood
The Nab
Stay Farm
Kepwick
Jaques Wood
135
Quarry (dis)
Thwaites Farm
Sorrow Beck
Moor House
Honeykiln Farm
Bridge Beck Lane
139
Thwaites Lane
Hunter's Hill
186
Quarries (dis)
201
169
Manor House Farm
Bridge Beck
Cowling
CP
Knipe

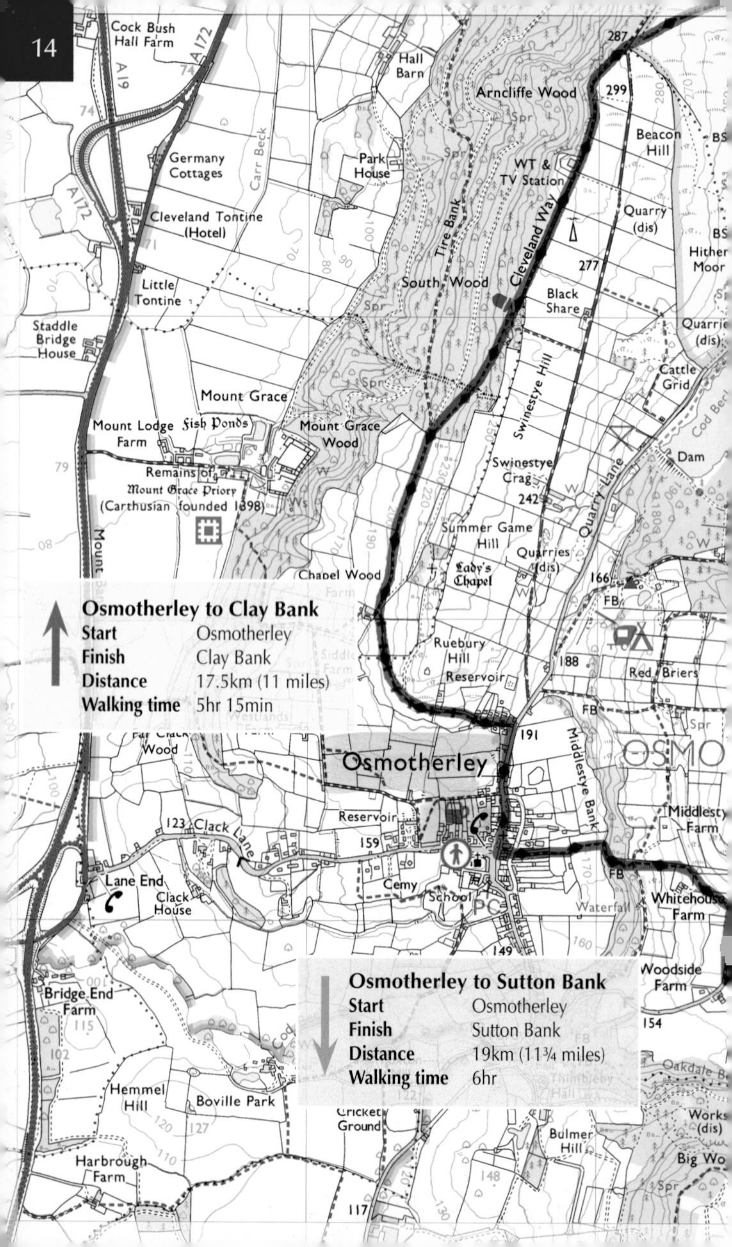

Osmotherley to Clay Bank

Start	Osmotherley
Finish	Clay Bank
Distance	17.5km (11 miles)
Walking time	5hr 15min

Osmotherley to Sutton Bank

Start	Osmotherley
Finish	Sutton Bank
Distance	19km (11¾ miles)
Walking time	6hr

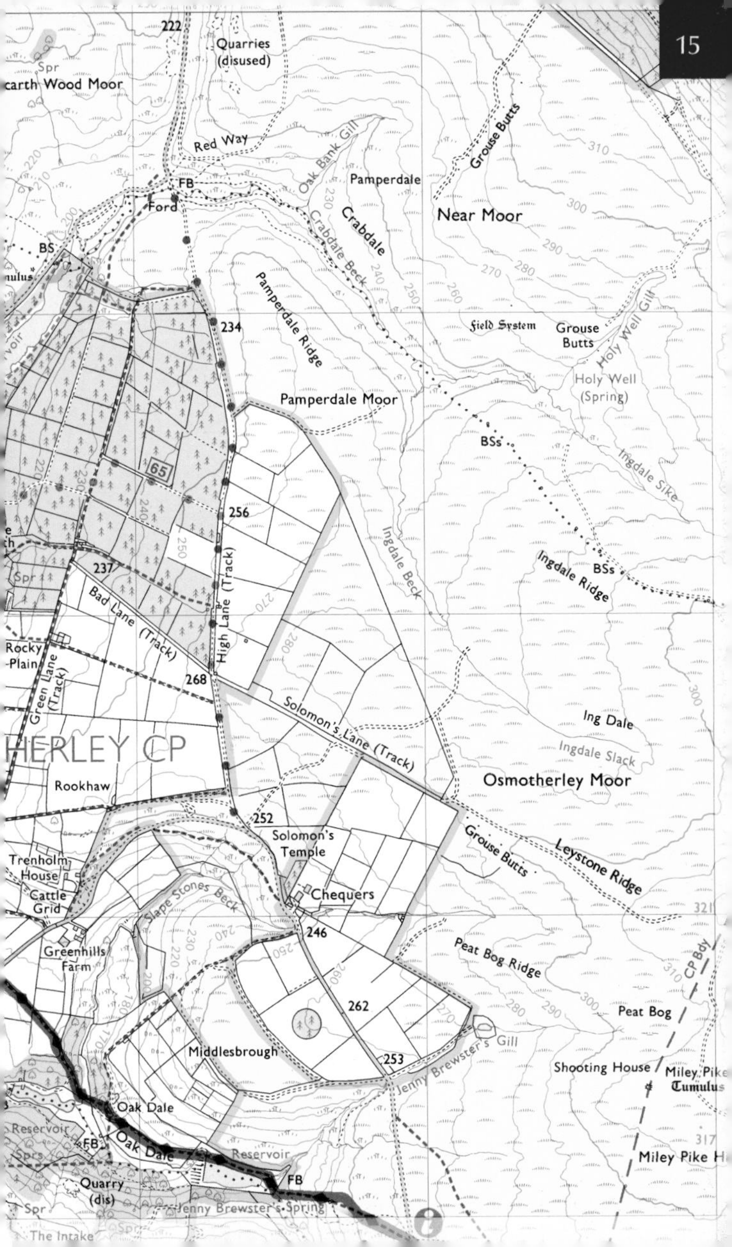
222
Quarries
(disused)
Spr
carth Wood Moor
Red Way
Oak Bank Gill
Pamperdale
Grouse Butts
310
FB
Ford
Crabdale
Near Moor
300
Crabdale Beck
290
BS
Pamperdale Ridge
270
280
260
250
240
230
234
Field System
Grouse
Butts
Holy Well Gill
Holy Well
(Spring)
Pamperdale Moor
BSs
Ingdale Sike
65
256
Ingdale Beck
237
Spr
High Lane (Track)
Ingdale Ridge
BSs
Bad Lane (Track)
Rocky
Plain
Green Lane
(Track)
268
Solomon's Lane (Track)
Ing Dale
Ingdale Slack
HERLEY CP
Rookhaw
Osmotherley Moor
252
Solomon's
Temple
Trenholm
House
Cattle
Grid
Grouse Butts
Leystone Ridge
Slape Stones Beck
Chequers
246
321
Greenhills
Farm
Peat Bog Ridge
CP Bdy
262
Peat Bog
Middlesbrough
253
Jenny Brewster's Gill
Shooting House
Miley Pike
Tumulus
Oak Dale
Reservoir
FB
Oak Dale
Reservoir
Sprs
317
Miley Pike H
FB
Quarry
(dis)
Spr
Jenny Brewster's Spring
The Intake

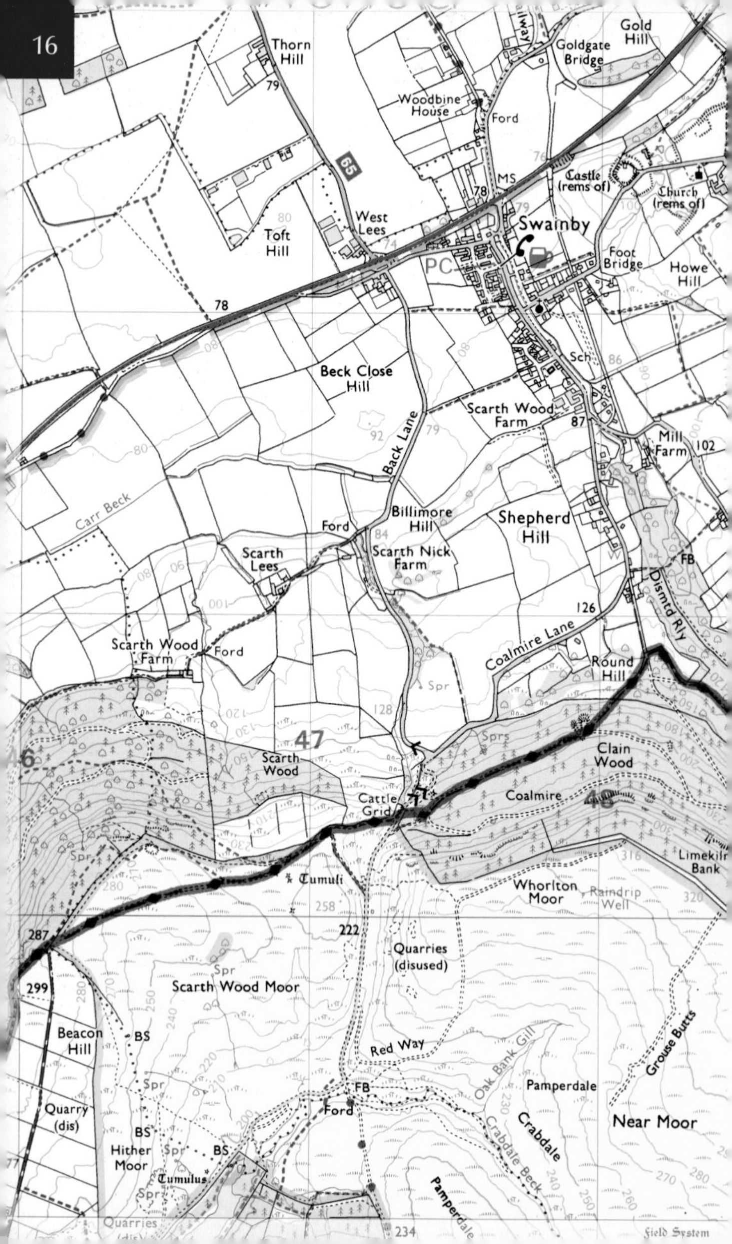
Thorn Hill
Gold Hill
Goldgate Bridge
Woodbine House
Ford
Castle (rems of)
Church (rems of)
MS
Swainby
West Lees
Toft Hill
PC
Foot Bridge
Howe Hill
Sch
Beck Close Hill
Scarth Wood Farm
Back Lane
Mill Farm
Carr Beck
Billimore Hill
Shepherd Hill
Ford
Scarth Lees
Scarth Nick Farm
Dismtd Rly
FB
Coalmire Lane
Scarth Wood Farm
Ford
Round Hill
Spr
Sprs
Scarth Wood
Clain Wood
Cattle Grid
Coalmire
Limekiln Bank
Tumuli
Whorlton Moor
Raindrip Well
Quarries (disused)
Scarth Wood Moor
Beacon Hill
BS
Red Way
Oak Bank Gill
Grouse Butts
Pamperdale
FB
Ford
Quarry (dis)
Hither Moor
Tumulus
Crabdale
Crabdale Beck
Near Moor
Pamperdale
Quarries
Field System

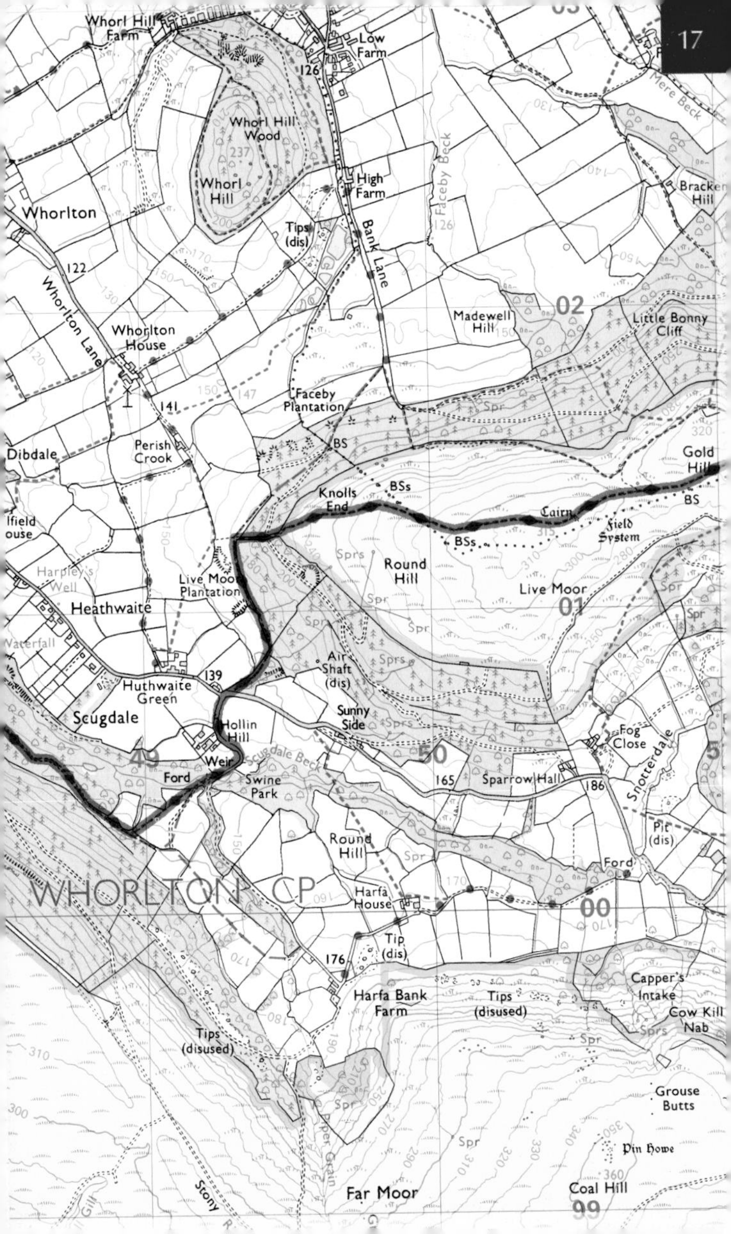
Whorl Hill Farm
Low Farm
126
Mere Beck
Whorl Hill Wood
237
Whorl Hill
High Farm
Faceby Beck
Bracken Hill
Whorlton
Tips (dis)
Bank Lane
122
Whorlton Lane
02
Madewell Hill
Little Bonny Cliff
Whorlton House
Faceby Plantation
141
147
Spr
320
Dibdale
Perish Crook
BS
Gold Hill
Knolls End
BSs
Cairn
Field System
lfield ouse
BSs
Round Hill
Live Moor
Harpley's Well
Live Moor Plantation
01
Heathwaite
Spr
Sprs
Waterfall
Air Shaft (dis)
Huthwaite Green
139
Scugdale
Sunny Side
Hollin Hill
Fog Close
Snotterdale
49
Weir
Scugdale Beck
50
Ford
Swine Park
165
Sparrow Hall
186
Pit (dis)
Round Hill
Ford
WHORLTON CP
Harfa House
00
Tip (dis)
176
Harfa Bank Farm
Tips (disused)
Capper's Intake
Cow Kill Nab
Tips (disused)
Grouse Butts
Pin Howe
Piper Grain
Far Moor
Coal Hill
Stony
Gill
99

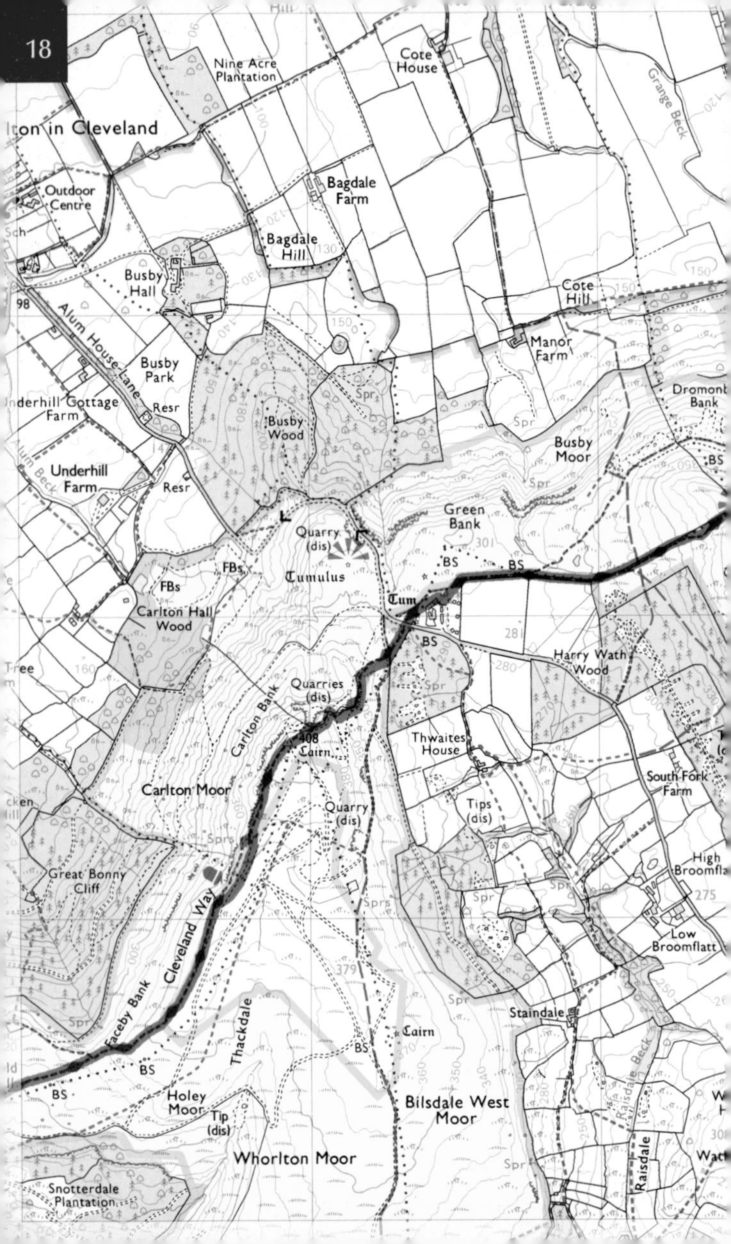
Nine Acre Plantation
Cote House
Grange Beck
lton in Cleveland
Outdoor Centre
Sch
Bagdale Farm
Bagdale Hill
Busby Hall
Alum House Lane
Cote Hill
Manor Farm
Busby Park
Underhill Cottage Farm
Resr
Busby Wood
Spr
Dromonby Bank
Busby Moor
Alum Beck
Underhill Farm
Green Bank
Quarry (dis)
BS
Tumulus
FBs
Cum
Carlton Hall Wood
Harry Wath Wood
Quarries (dis)
Carlton Bank
408
Cairn
Thwaites House
South Fork Farm
Carlton Moor
Tips (dis)
Great Bonny Cliff
High Broomflat
Low Broomflatt
Cleveland Way
Faceby Bank
Staindale
Thackdale
Raisdale Beck
Holey Moor
Tip (dis)
Bilsdale West Moor
Whorlton Moor
Raisdale
Snotterdale Plantation

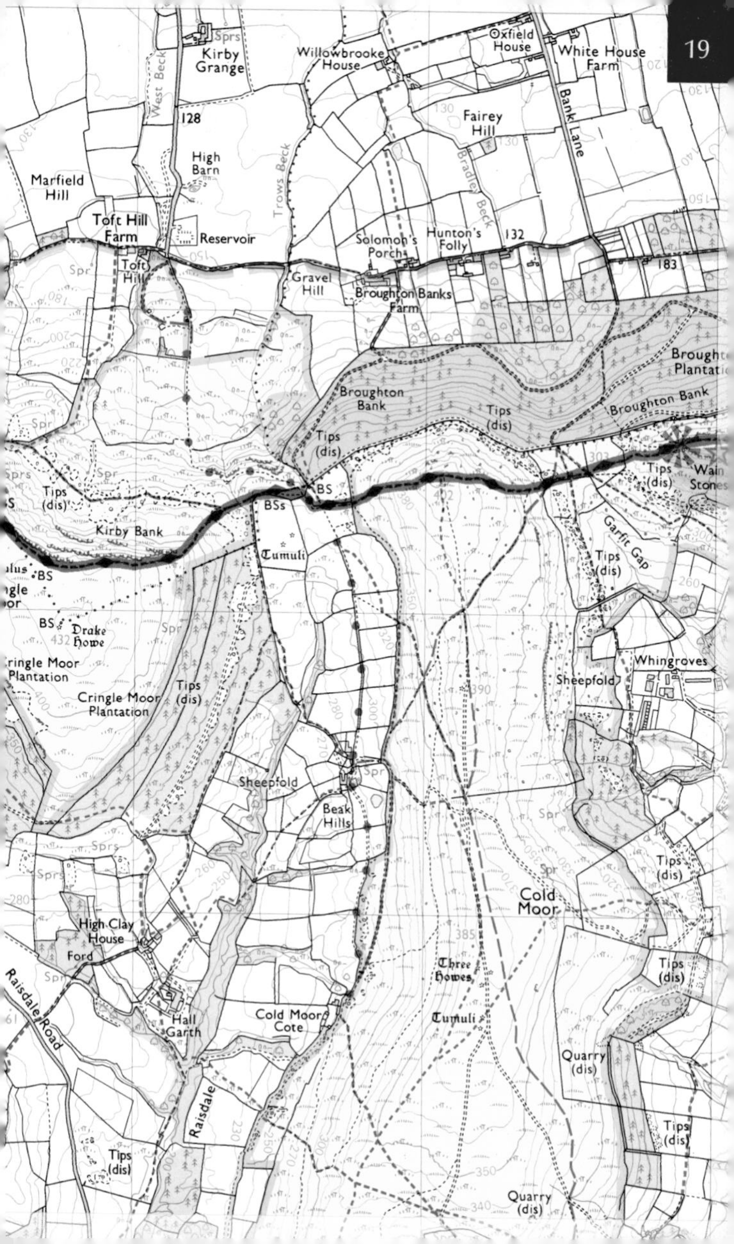
Kirby Grange
Willowbrooke House
Oxfield House
White House Farm
West Beck
128
Trows Beck
Fairey Hill
Bank Lane
Bradley Beck
Marfield Hill
High Barn
Toft Hill Farm
Reservoir
Solomon's Porch
Hunton's Folly
132
183
Toft Hill
Gravel Hill
Broughton Banks Farm
Broughton Plantation
Broughton Bank
Broughton Bank
Tips (dis)
Tips (dis)
Wain Stones
Tips (dis)
Kirby Bank
BS
BSs
Tumuli
Garfit Gap
Tips (dis)
Drake Howe
432
Cringle Moor Plantation
Cringle Moor Plantation
Tips (dis)
Whingroves
Sheepfold
Sheepfold
Beak Hills
Cold Moor
High Clay House
Ford
Raisdale Road
Hall Garth
Cold Moor Cote
Three Howes
Tumuli
Quarry (dis)
Raisdale
Tips (dis)
Tips (dis)
Tips (dis)
Tips (dis)
Quarry (dis)

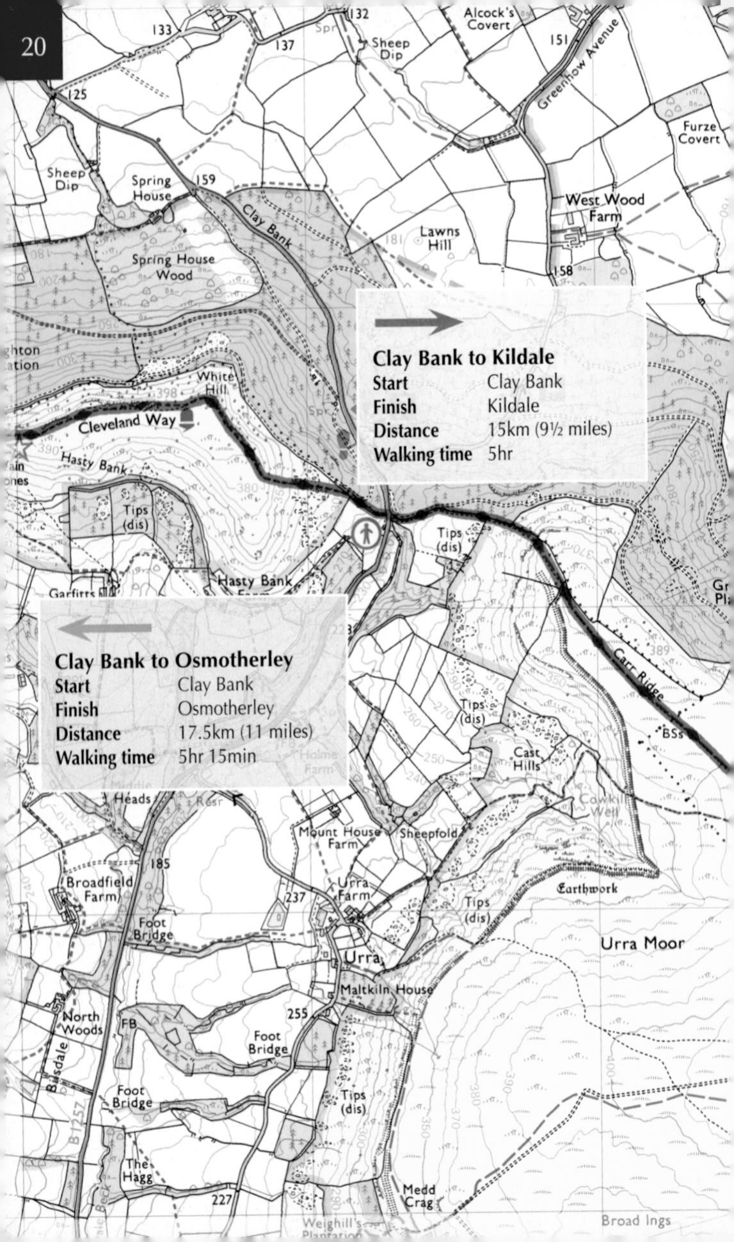

Clay Bank to Kildale

Start	Clay Bank
Finish	Kildale
Distance	15km (9½ miles)
Walking time	5hr

Clay Bank to Osmotherley

Start	Clay Bank
Finish	Osmotherley
Distance	17.5km (11 miles)
Walking time	5hr 15min

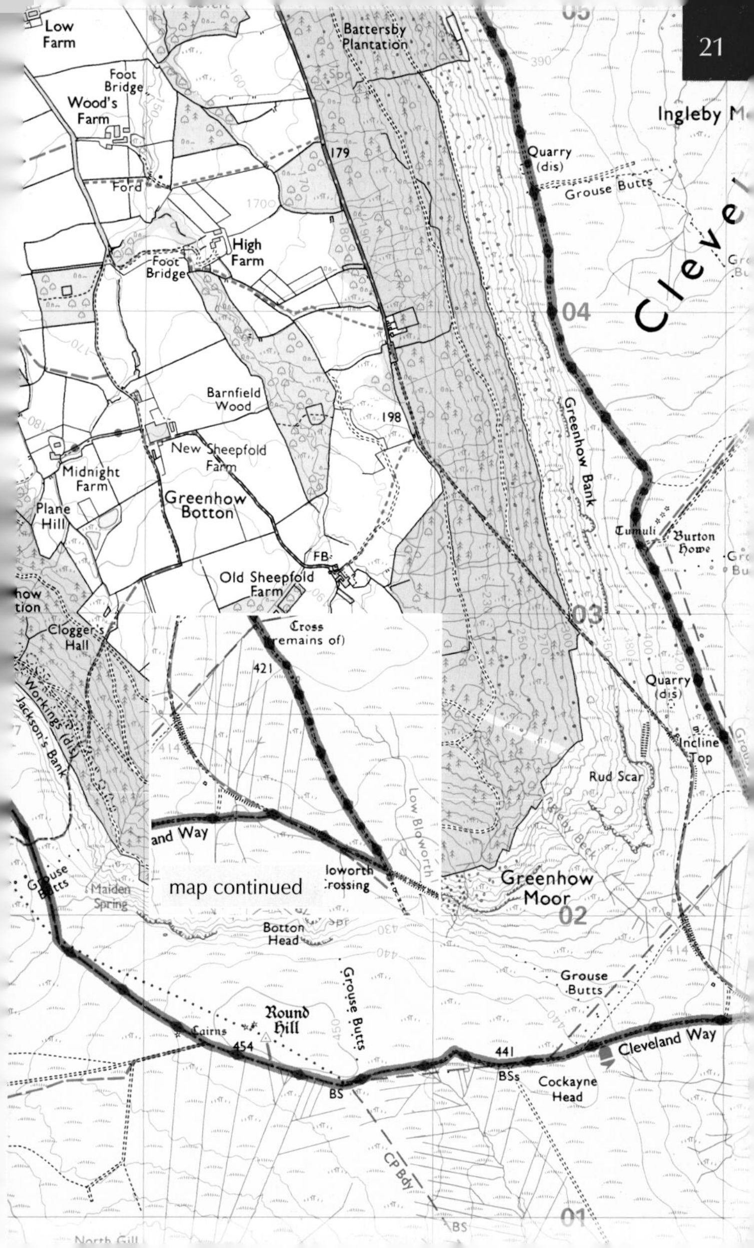
Low Farm
Battersby Plantation
Foot Bridge
Wood's Farm
Ingleby M
Quarry (dis)
Grouse Butts
Ford
High Farm
Foot Bridge
Cleve
Barnfield Wood
198
Greenhow Bank
New Sheepfold Farm
Midnight Farm
Greenhow Botton
Plane Hill
Tumuli
Burton Howe
FB
Old Sheepfold Farm
Clogger's Hall
Cross (remains of)
421
Jackson's Bank
Workings (dis)
Quarry (dis)
Incline Top
Rud Scar
Low Blaworth
Ingleby Beck
Greenhow Moor
Grouse Butts
Maiden Spring
Botton Head
Grouse Butts
Round Hill
Cairns
454
441
Cleveland Way
BS
BSs
Cockayne Head
CP Bdy
North Gill

map continued

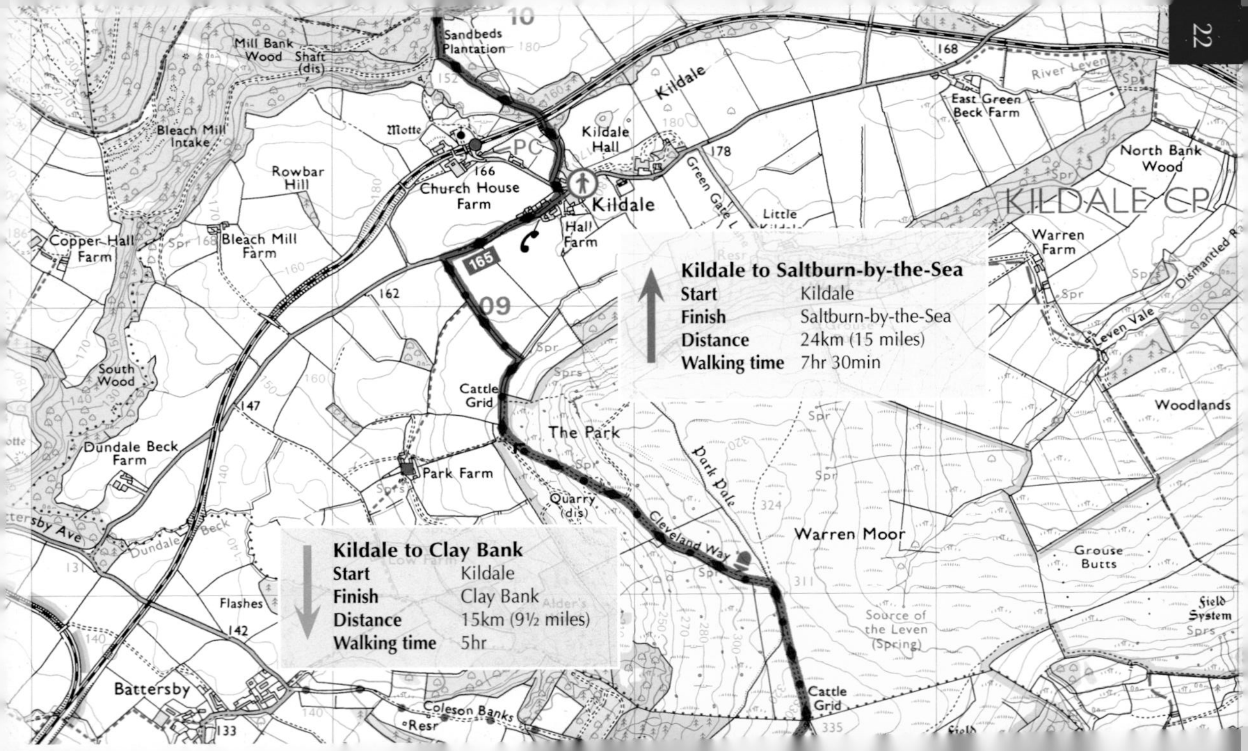

Kildale to Saltburn-by-the-Sea

Start	Kildale
Finish	Saltburn-by-the-Sea
Distance	24km (15 miles)
Walking time	7hr 30min

Kildale to Clay Bank

Start	Kildale
Finish	Clay Bank
Distance	15km (9½ miles)
Walking time	5hr

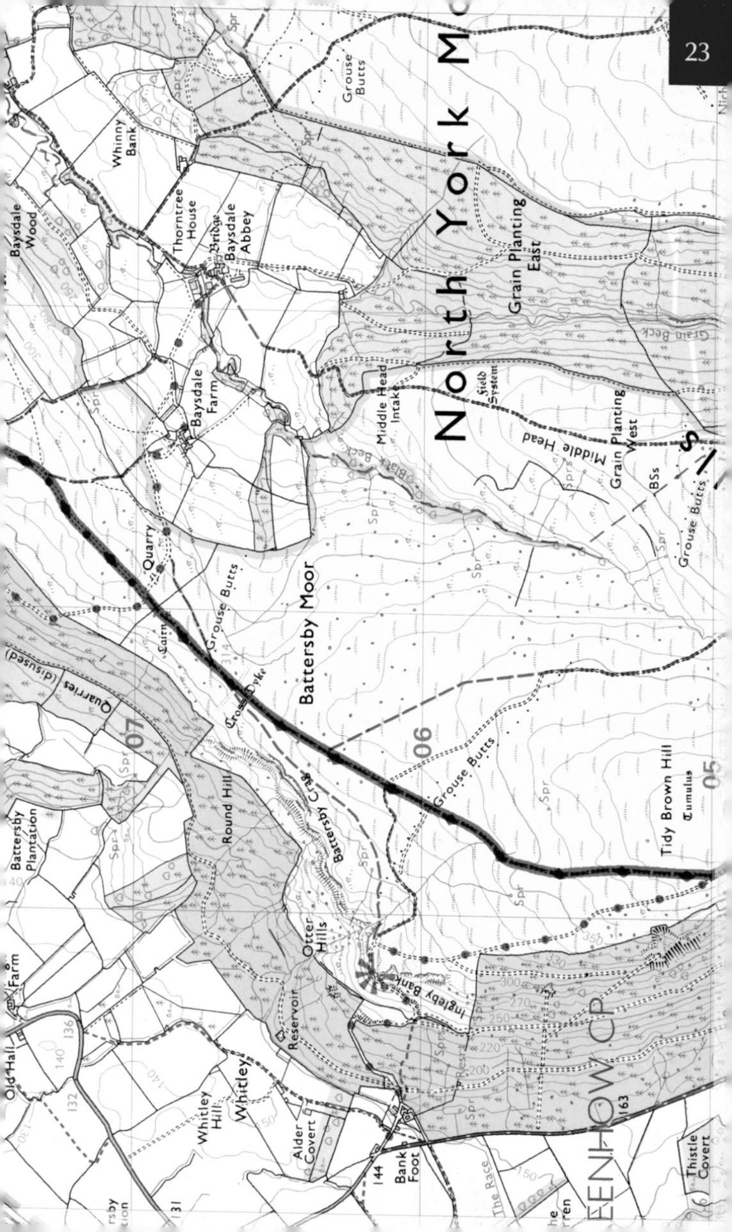
North York M
Baysdale Wood
Whinny Bank
Thorntree House
Bridge
Baysdale Abbey
Baysdale Farm
Grouse Butts
Middle Head Intake
Field System
Grain Planting East
Grain Beck
Grain Planting West
Middle Head
Black Beck
BSs
Grouse Butts
Quarry
Cairn
Grouse Butts
Battersby Moor
Cross Dyke
Quarries (disused)
07
06
05
Round Hill
Battersby Crag
Battersby Plantation
Grouse Butts
Tidy Brown Hill
Tumulus
Otter Hills
Reservoir
Ingleby Bank
Farm
Old Hall
Whitley Hill
Whitley
Alder Covert
Bank Foot
The Race
Thistle Covert
EENHOW CP

Tees Link
Kemplah Wood
Cairn
Hutton Village
Shaft (dis)
Hill Plain
Reed's Wood
Bold Venture Gill
Codhill Slack
The Race
Black Nab
Hutton Wood
Hutton Hall
Hutton Gate
Home Farm
Blue Lake Wood
Air Shaft (disused)
Hutton Moor
Hutton Lowcross Woods
Hanging Stone
Hanging Stone Wood
Newton Moor
Bousdale Wood
High Bousdale Wood
Cairns
Cleveland Way
Bousdale Hill
Bousdale Farm
Mount House Farm
Roseberry Common
Pinchinthorpe House
High Farm
Newton under Roseberry
Rye Banks
Brant Gate (Path)
Roseberry Well
Roseberry
Ward's Belt
Pinchinthorpe Hall
Green Hills
Hall Hill
Roseberry Lane

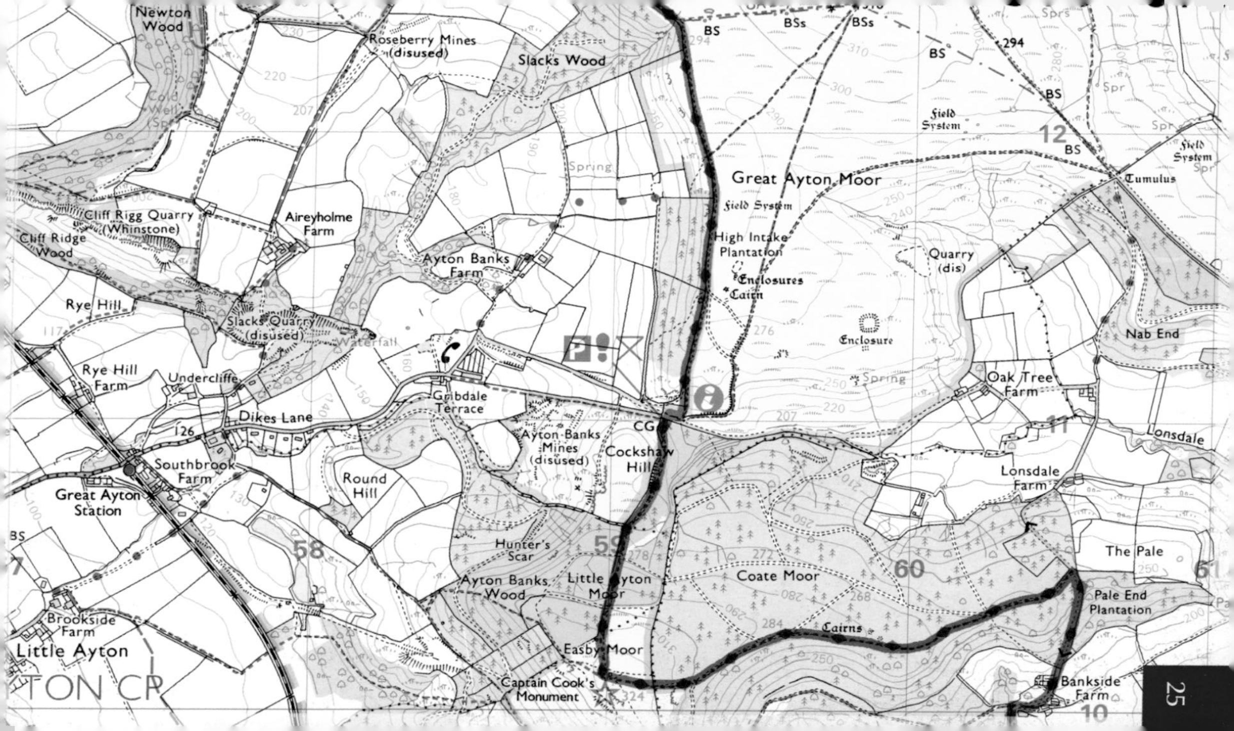
Newton Wood
Roseberry Mines (disused)
Slacks Wood
Great Ayton Moor
Field System
High Intake Plantation
Enclosures
Cairn
Enclosure
Spring
Quarry (dis)
Tumulus
Nab End
Cliff Rigg Quarry (Whinstone)
Cliff Ridge Wood
Aireyholme Farm
Ayton Banks Farm
Rye Hill
Slacks Quarry (disused)
Waterfall
Rye Hill Farm
Undercliffe
Gribdale Terrace
Dikes Lane
Oak Tree Farm
Lonsdale
Lonsdale Farm
CG
Ayton Banks Mines (disused)
Cockshaw Hill
Southbrook Farm
Great Ayton Station
Round Hill
Hunter's Scar
Ayton Banks Wood
Little Ayton Moor
Coate Moor
Cairns
The Pale
Pale End Plantation
Easby Moor
Captain Cook's Monument
Bankside Farm
Brookside Farm
Little Ayton
TON CP

The Duck
Peregrine Plantation
Mucky Lane (Track)
Waterfall Gill
Waterfall Wood
School
Sch
Horse Parks Wood
Waterfall Farm
Colleges
Hospl
Gisborough Hall
Whitby Lane
Gisborough Priory (remains of)
MP
Cleveland Street
Little Waterfall Farm
168
PO
94
GUISBOROUGH
Butt Lane
Foxdale Farm
Dismtd Rly
Belmont Farm
Old Park Farm
Brown Hill
Cow Pasture Hill
Schs
West Banks
Belman Bank
Shaft (dis)
Quarry (dis)
Guisborough Woods
126
Spring Wood
Shaft (dis)
Highcliff Wood
Highcliff Nab
Cairn
324
Cairn
319
Highcliff Gate Spring
Cairn
Grouse Butts
Westworth Wood
hcliffe Farm
Grouse Butts (disused)
Cairn
Three Howes
284
Grouse Butts
Bethal Slack

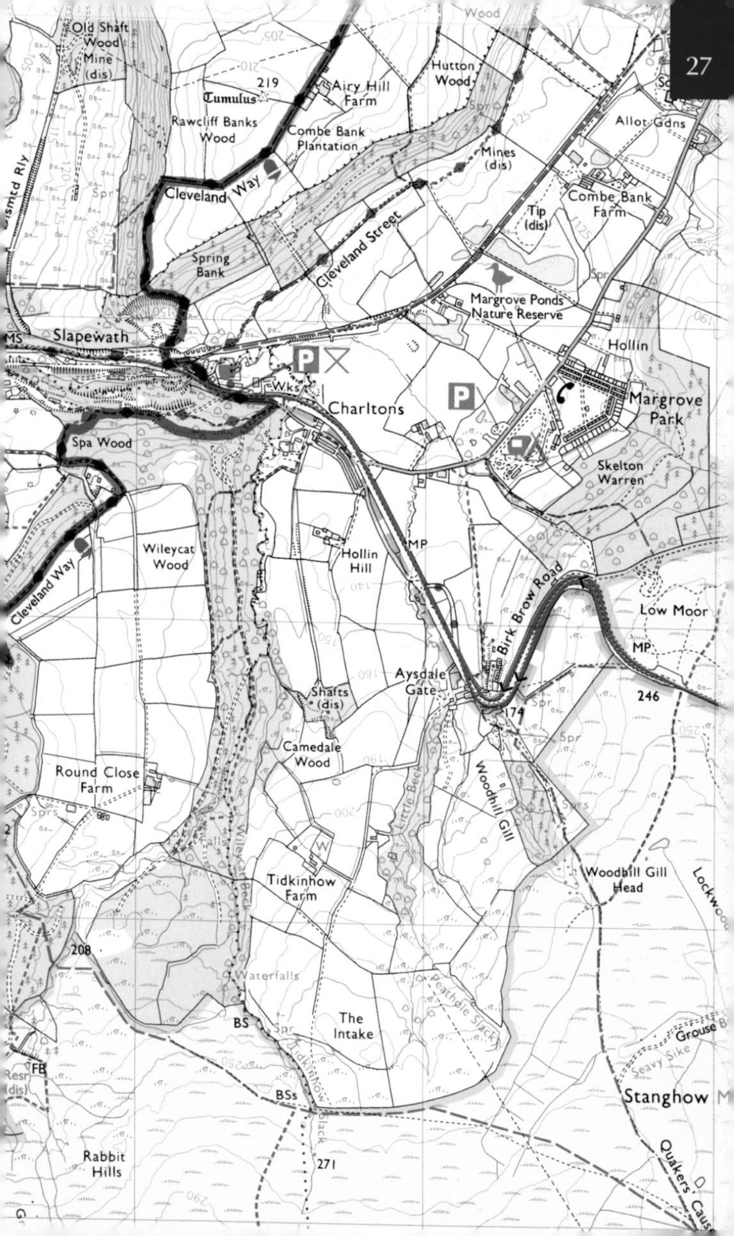
Old Shaft
Wood
Mine
(dis)
219
Tumulus
Airy Hill
Farm
Hutton
Wood
Wood
Rawcliff Banks
Wood
Combe Bank
Plantation
Cleveland Way
Mines
(dis)
Allot Gdns
Combe Bank
Farm
Tip
(dis)
Cleveland Street
Spring
Bank
Margrove Ponds
Nature Reserve
Slapewath
MS
Hollin
Wks
Charltons
Margrove
Park
Spa Wood
Skelton
Warren
Wileycat
Wood
Hollin
Hill
MP
Cleveland Way
Birk Brow Road
Low Moor
MP
246
Aysdale
Gate
174
Shafts
(dis)
Camedale
Wood
Round Close
Farm
Sprs
Woodhill
Gill
Falls
Wileycat Beck
Little Beck
Tidkinhow
Farm
Woodhill Gill
Head
Lockwood
208
Waterfalls
Peathole Slack
The
Intake
BS
Spr
Grouse
Seavy Sike
FB
Resr
(dis)
BSs
Tidkinhow Slack
Stanghow
271
Rabbit
Hills
Quakers' Causeway

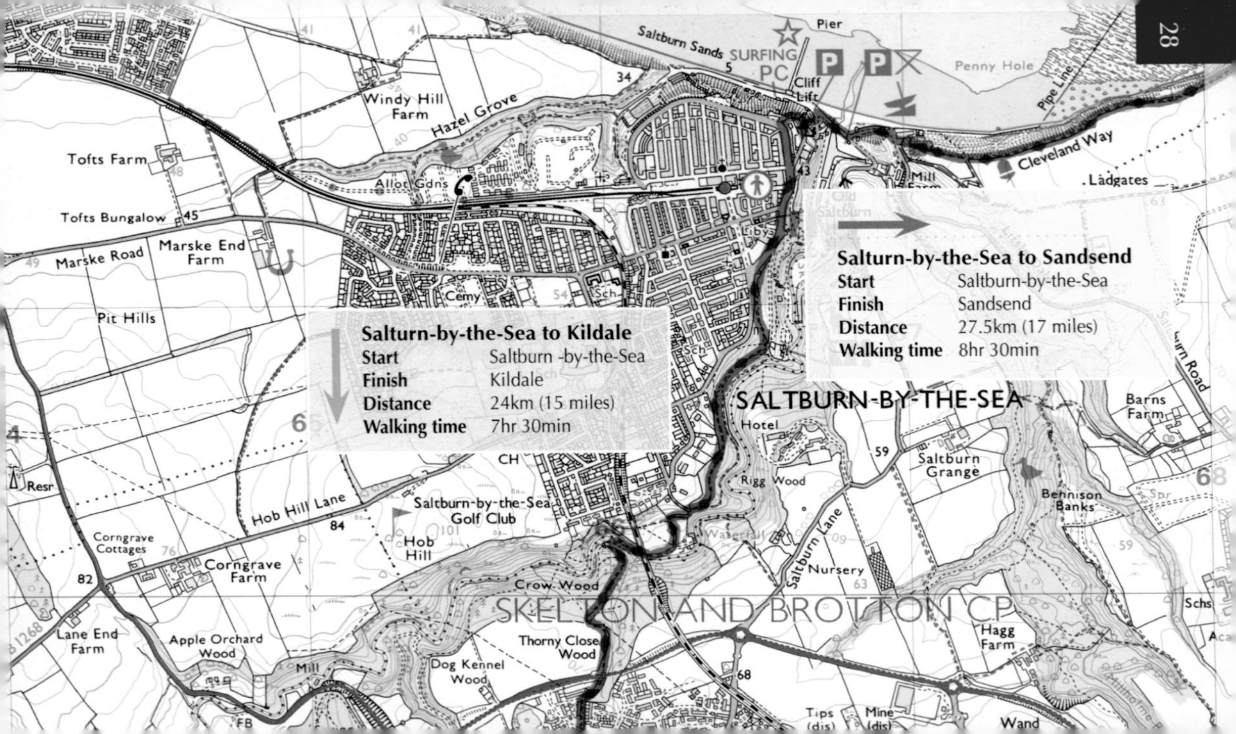
Salturn-by-the-Sea to Sandsend
Start Saltburn-by-the-Sea
Finish Sandsend
Distance 27.5km (17 miles)
Walking time 8hr 30min
Salturn-by-the-Sea to Kildale
Start Saltburn -by-the-Sea
Finish Kildale
Distance 24km (15 miles)
Walking time 7hr 30min
SALTBURN-BY-THE-SEA
SKELTON AND BROTTON CP
Saltburn Sands
Pier
SURFING
PC
Cliff Lift
Penny Hole
Pipe Line
Cleveland Way
Ladgates
Mill Farm
Old Saltburn
Windy Hill Farm
Hazel Grove
Tofts Farm
Allot Gdns
Tofts Bungalow
Marske End Farm
Marske Road
Cemy
Sch
Liby
Pit Hills
Saltburn Road
Barns Farm
Hotel
Saltburn Grange
Rigg Wood
Bennison Banks
CH
Saltburn-by-the-Sea Golf Club
Hob Hill Lane
Hob Hill
Resr
Corngrave Cottages
Corngrave Farm
Waterfall
Saltburn Lane
Nursery
Crow Wood
Schs
Hagg Farm
Lane End Farm
Apple Orchard Wood
Thorny Close Wood
Dog Kennel Wood
Mill
FB
Tips (dis)
Mine (dis)
Wand

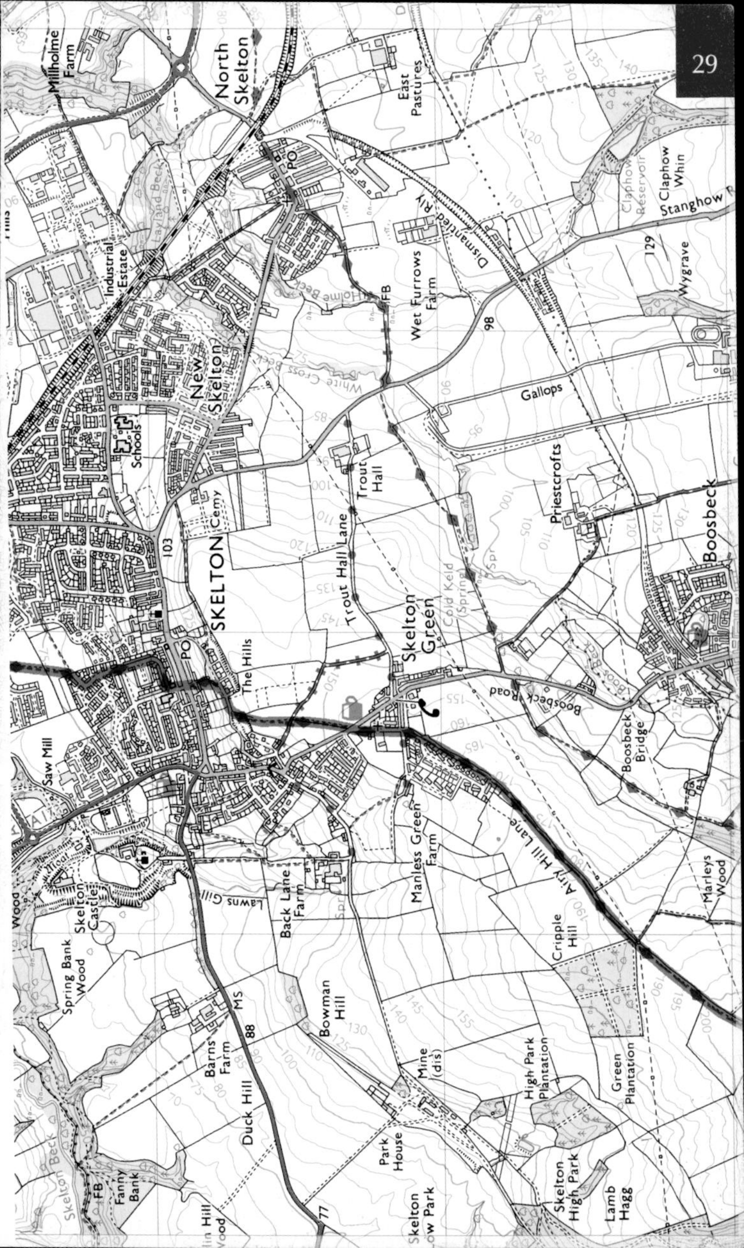
North Skelton
Millholme Farm
East Pastures
PO
Claphow Reservoir
Claphow Whin
Stanghow R
Dismantled Rly
Industrial Estate
Layland Beck
Holme Beck
FB
Wet Furrows Farm
129
Wygrave
98
New Skelton
White Cross Beck
Gallops
Schools
Trout Hall
Cemy
Priestcrofts
Boosbeck
103
SKELTON
Trout Hall Lane
The Hills
Skelton Green
Cold Keld (Spring)
Spr
PO
Boosbeck Road
Boosbeck Beck
Boosbeck Bridge
Saw Mill
A173
Moat
Skelton Castle
Lawns Gill
Back Lane Farm
Manless Green Farm
Airy Hill Lane
Marleys Wood
Cripple Hill
Wood
Spring Bank Wood
MS
88
Bowman Hill
Barns Farm
Mine (dis)
High Park Plantation
Green Plantation
Duck Hill
Park House
Skelton Beck
FB
Fanny Bank
Hill Wood
77
Skelton Low Park
Skelton High Park
Lamb Hagg

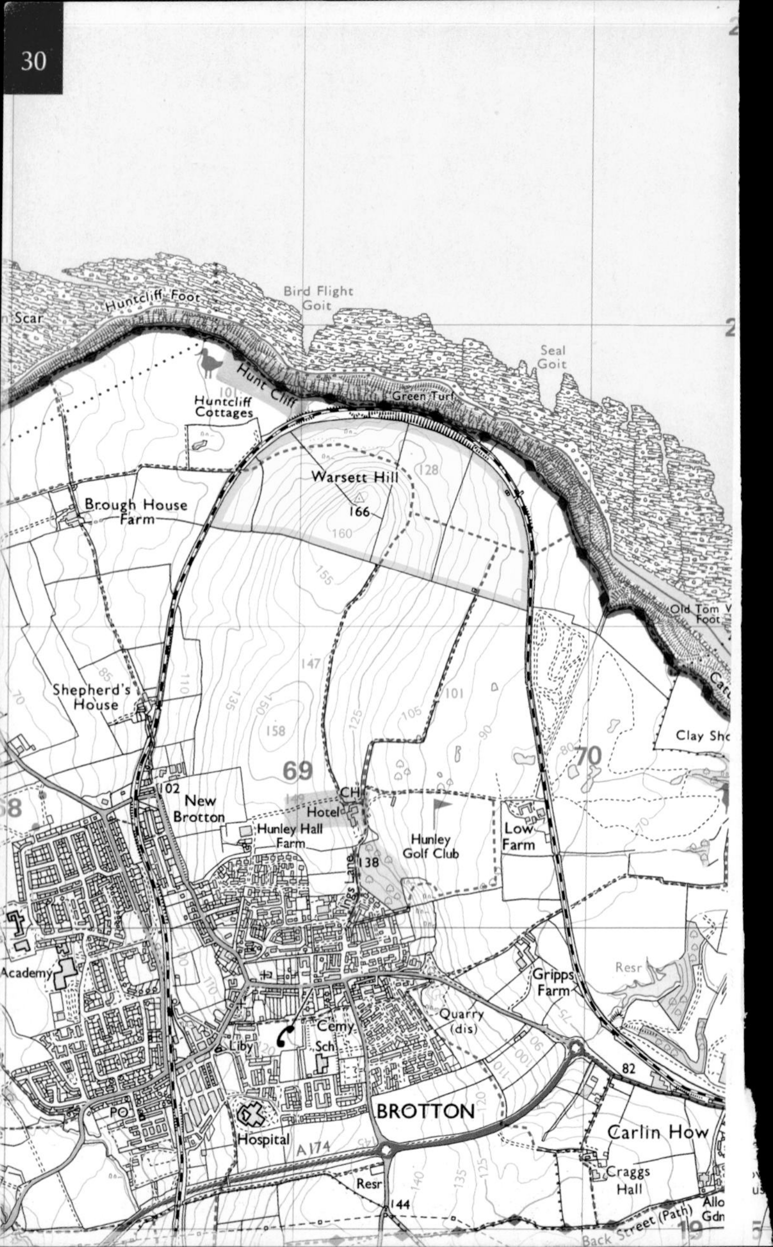
Huntcliff Foot
Scar
Bird Flight Goit
Seal Goit
Hunt Cliff
Green Turf
Huntcliff Cottages
Warsett Hill
166
128
160
155
Brough House Farm
Old Tom Foot
147
Shepherd's House
158
101
105
125
135
150
110
85
70
90
80
Clay
70
69
68
CH
Hotel
New Brotton
102
Hunley Hall Farm
Hunley Golf Club
Low Farm
138
Ings Lane
Academy
Resr
Gripps Farm
Quarry (dis)
Cemy
Sch
Liby
PO
BROTTON
Hospital
A174
82
Carlin How
Craggs Hall
Resr
144
Back Street (Path)
Allo Gdn
19

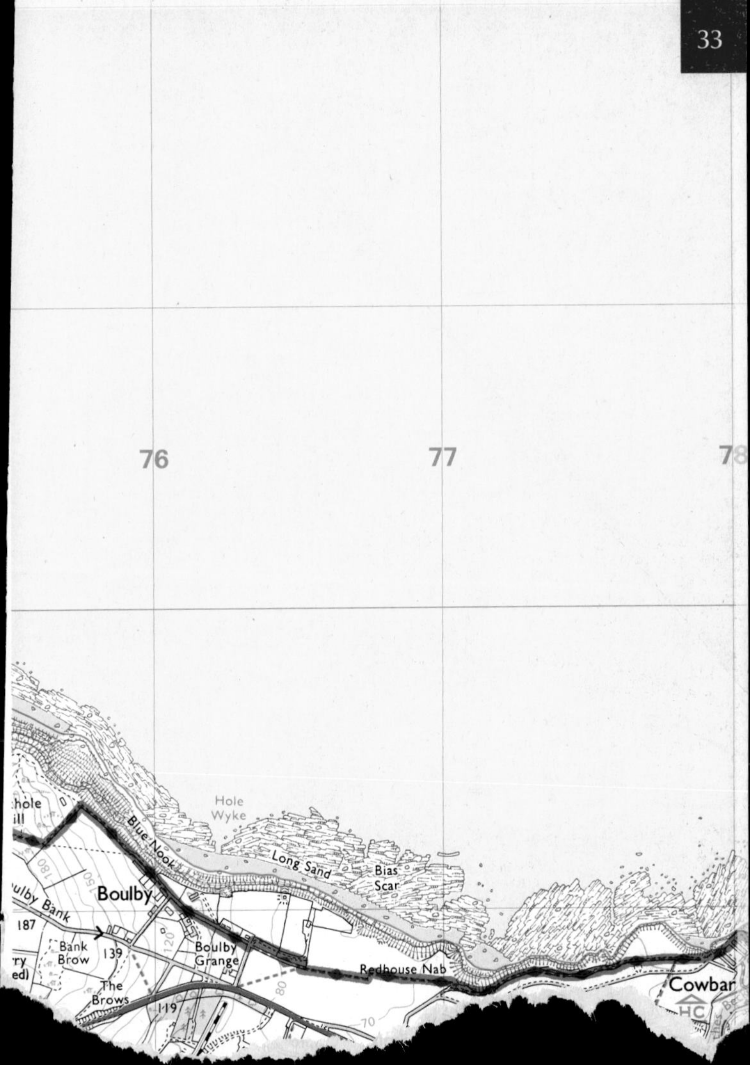
76
77
Hole
Wyke
Blue Nook
Long Sand
Bias
Scar
Boulby
187
Bank
Brow
139
Boulby
Grange
The
Brows
119
Redhouse Nab
Cowbar
180
150
120
80
70

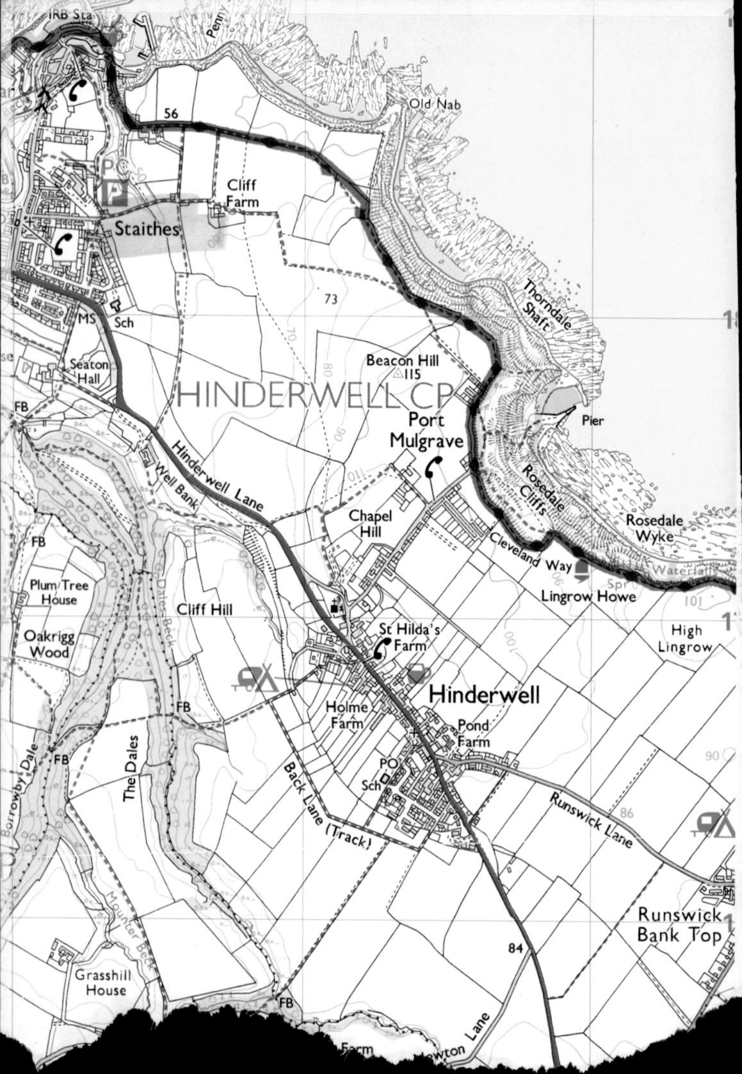
IRB Sta
Jet Wyke
Old Nab
56
Cliff Farm
Staithes
73
MS
Sch
Seaton Hall
HINDERWELL CP
Beacon Hill
115
Thorndale Shaft
Port Mulgrave
Pier
FB
Hinderwell Lane
Well Bank
Chapel Hill
Cleveland Way
Rosedale Cliffs
Rosedale Wyke
Waterfalls
Lingrow Howe
High Lingrow
Plum Tree House
Oakrigg Wood
Cliff Hill
Dales Beck
St Hilda's Farm
Hinderwell
Holme Farm
Pond Farm
PO
Sch
Back Lane (Track)
Runswick Lane
86
90
101
Runswick Bank Top
84
The Dales
Borrowby Dale
Mounter Beck
Grasshill House
Farm

Lingrow
Knock
MLW
ngrow Cliffs
Wrack
Hills
Cobble
Dump
Jarvis'
Landing Hole
Runswick Bay
P
PC
Hotel
IRB Sta
Runswick
Bay
Nettle Dale
P
Dother
Pits
Runswick
Sands
Spr
Dunsley Dale
Hob
Holes
Waterfalls
Spr
High
Cliff
103
Kettleness Mines
(disused)
Shaft
(dis)
Butter
howe
Spr
Sprs
93
Kettleness
Farm
Hill
Stones
Kettleness
Sand
Waterfall
123
99

Sandsend to Salturn-by-the-Sea

Start	Sandsend
Finish	Saltburn-by-the-Sea
Distance	27.5km (17 miles)
Walking time	8hr 30min

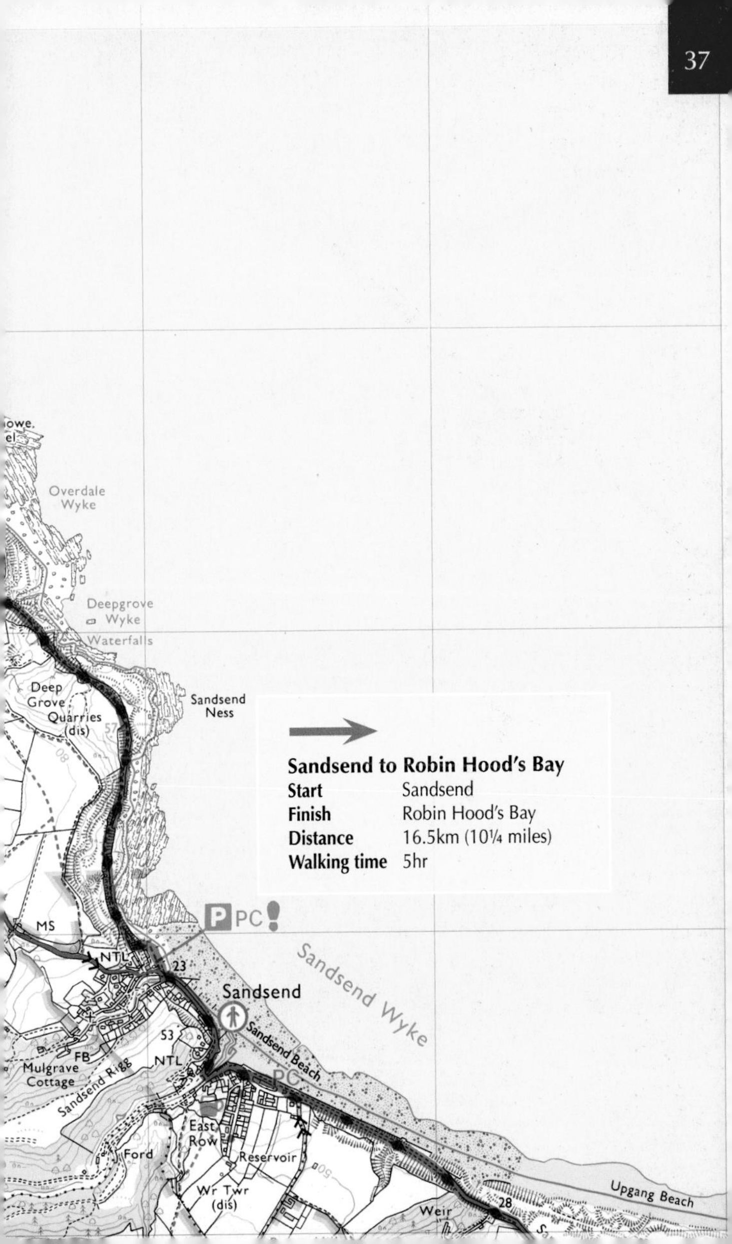
Overdale Wyke
Deepgrove Wyke
Waterfalls
Deep Grove Quarries (dis)
Sandsend Ness
Sandsend to Robin Hood's Bay
Start Sandsend
Finish Robin Hood's Bay
Distance 16.5km (10¼ miles)
Walking time 5hr
P PC
MS
NTL
23
Sandsend
Sandsend Wyke
Sandsend Beach
53
NTL
PC
FB
Mulgrave Cottage
Sandsend Rigg
East Row
Ford
Reservoir
Wr Twr (dis)
Weir
28
Upgang Beach

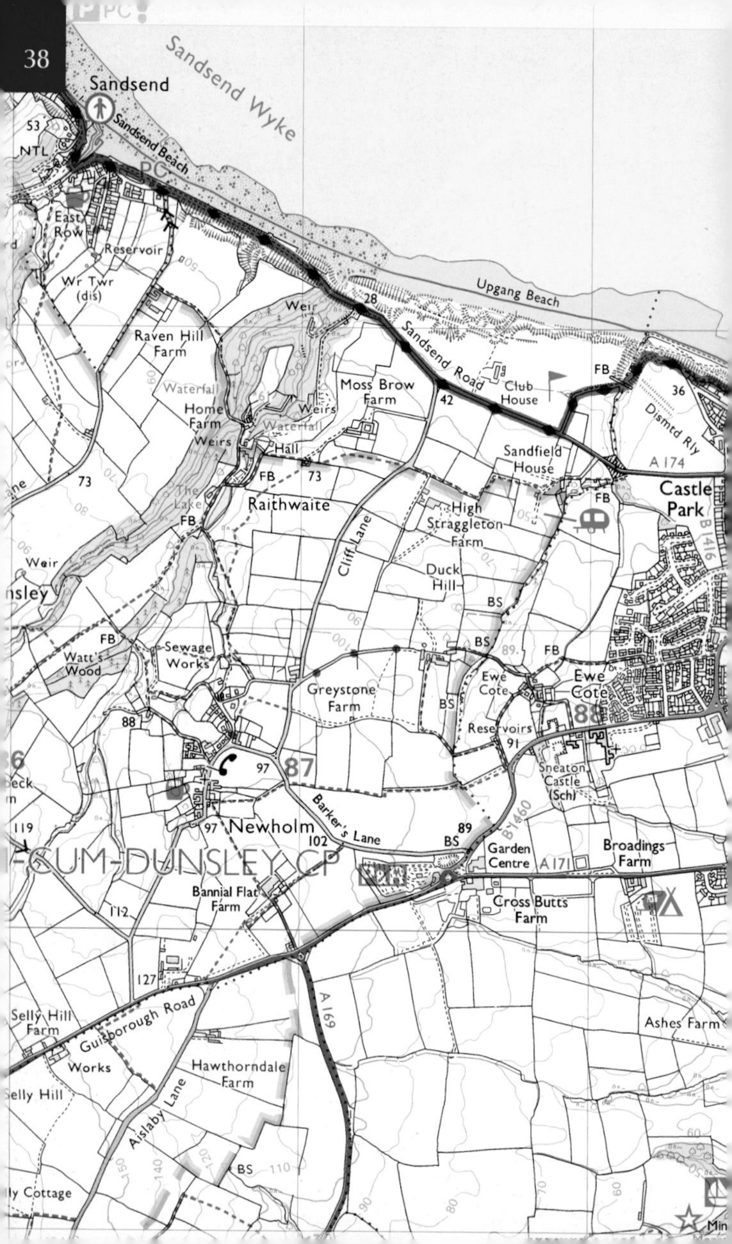
Sandsend
Sandsend Wyke
Sandsend Beach
PC
53
NTL
East Row
Reservoir
Wr Twr (dis)
Upgang Beach
28
Weir
Raven Hill Farm
Waterfall
Home Farm
Weirs
Moss Brow Farm
Weirs
Waterfall
Sandsend Road
Club House
42
FB
36
Dismtd Rly
Hall
FB
73
73
The Lake
Raithwaite
Sandfield House
A 174
Castle Park
FB
High Straggleton Farm
Cliff Lane
B 1416
Weir
Duck Hill
BS
BS
FB
Watt's Wood
Sewage Works
Greystone Farm
FB
Ewe Cote
Ewe Cote
88
BS
Reservoirs
91
88
97
87
Sneaton Castle (Sch)
Barker's Lane
119
97
Newholm
102
89
BS
B 1460
Garden Centre
A 171
Broadings Farm
CUM-DUNSLEY CP
Bannial Flat Farm
Cross Butts Farm
112
127
A 169
Ashes Farm
Selly Hill Farm
Guisborough Road
Works
Hawthorndale Farm
Selly Hill
Aislaby Lane
BS
lly Cottage

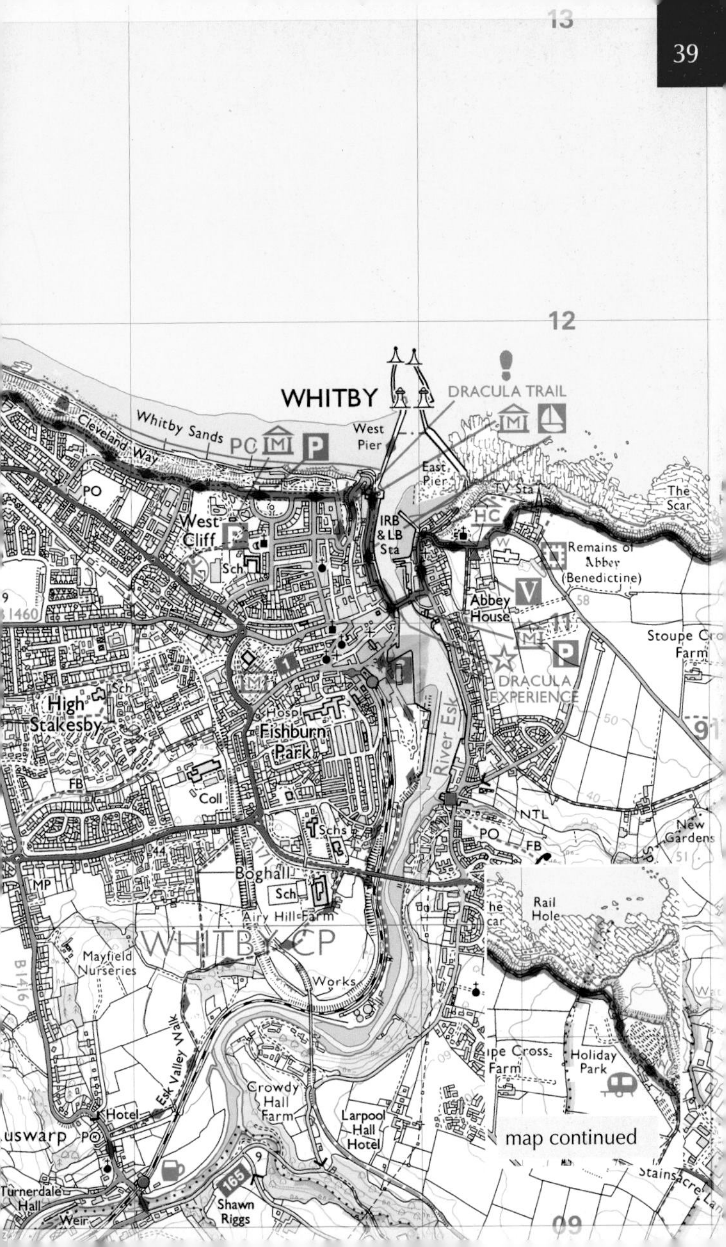
13
12
WHITBY
DRACULA TRAIL
Whitby Sands
Cleveland Way
PC
West Pier
East Pier
TV Sta
The Scar
PO
West Cliff
Sch
IRB & LB Sta
HC
Remains of Abbey (Benedictine)
Abbey House
58
Stoupe Cro
Farm
B1460
DRACULA EXPERIENCE
Sch
High Stakesby
Hospl
Fishburn Park
River Esk
50
91
FB
Coll
40
NTL
Schs
PO
FB
New Gardens
51
44
A171
Boghall
MP
Sch
Airy Hill Farm
The Scar
Rail Hole
WHITBY CP
Mayfield Nurseries
B1416
Works
Esk Valley Walk
ipe Cross Farm
Holiday Park
Crowdy Hall Farm
Hotel
Larpool Hall Hotel
uswarp
PO
map continued
165
Stainsacre Lane
Turnerdale Hall
Weir
Shawn Riggs
09

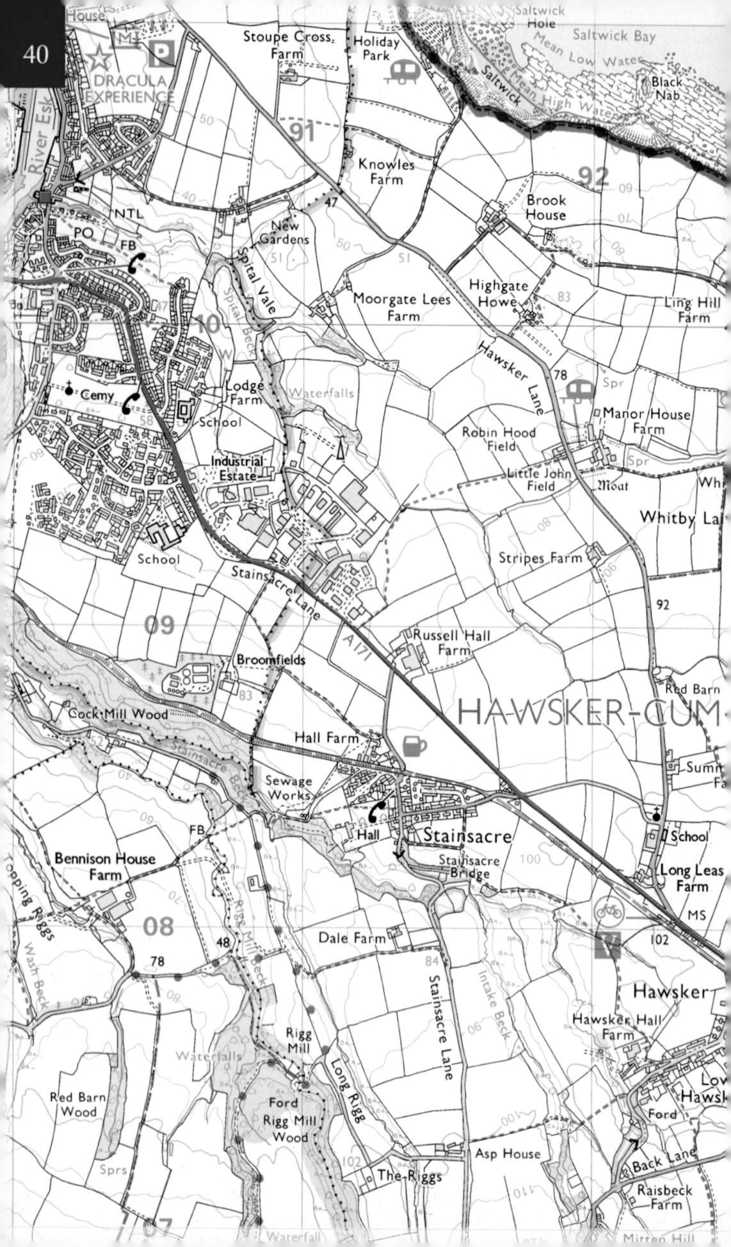
House
DRACULA EXPERIENCE
Stoupe Cross Farm
Holiday Park
Saltwick Hole
Saltwick Bay
Mean Low Water
Saltwick
Mean High Water
Black Nab
River Esk
91
92
Knowles Farm
Brook House
NTL
PO
FB
New Gardens
Spital Vale
Spital Beck
Moorgate Lees Farm
Highgate Howe
Ling Hill Farm
10
Hawsker Lane
Lodge Farm
Waterfalls
Cemy
School
Manor House Farm
Robin Hood Field
Industrial Estate
Little John Field
Moat
Whitby La
Stripes Farm
School
Stainsacre Lane
09
A171
Russell Hall Farm
Broomfields
Red Barn
HAWSKER-CUM
Cock Mill Wood
Stainsacre Beck
Hall Farm
Sewage Works
Summ Fa
Hall
Stainsacre
Stainsacre Bridge
School
Long Leas Farm
FB
Bennison House Farm
Topping Riggs
08
Rigg Mill Beck
Dale Farm
MS
Wash Beck
Stainsacre Lane
Intake Beck
Hawsker
Hawsker Hall Farm
Rigg Mill
Long Rigg
Waterfalls
Red Barn Wood
Ford
Rigg Mill Wood
Low Hawsk
Ford
Asp House
Back Lane
Sprs
The Riggs
Raisbeck Farm
07
Waterfall
Mitten Hill

93
94
95
Whitestone Point
Signal
59
97
Ling Hill
101
Beacon Hill
High Whitby
Pit (dis)
Laithes
Widdy Head
Widdy Field
STAINSACRE CP
Cleveland Way
109
Gnipe Howe
Maw Wyke Hole
FB
Pursglove Stye Batts
Oakham Wood
Oakham Beck
Pursglove Stye
Waterfalls
Hawsker Bottoms
Northcliffe Holiday Park
108
Limekiln Slack
Ford
Spr
White Horse
110
120
1
130
High Hawsker
Reservoir
Seaview
127
B1447
Hilda's Howe
East Close Beck
Raw Pasture Beck
Bottom House
Pits (dis)
143
House Lane

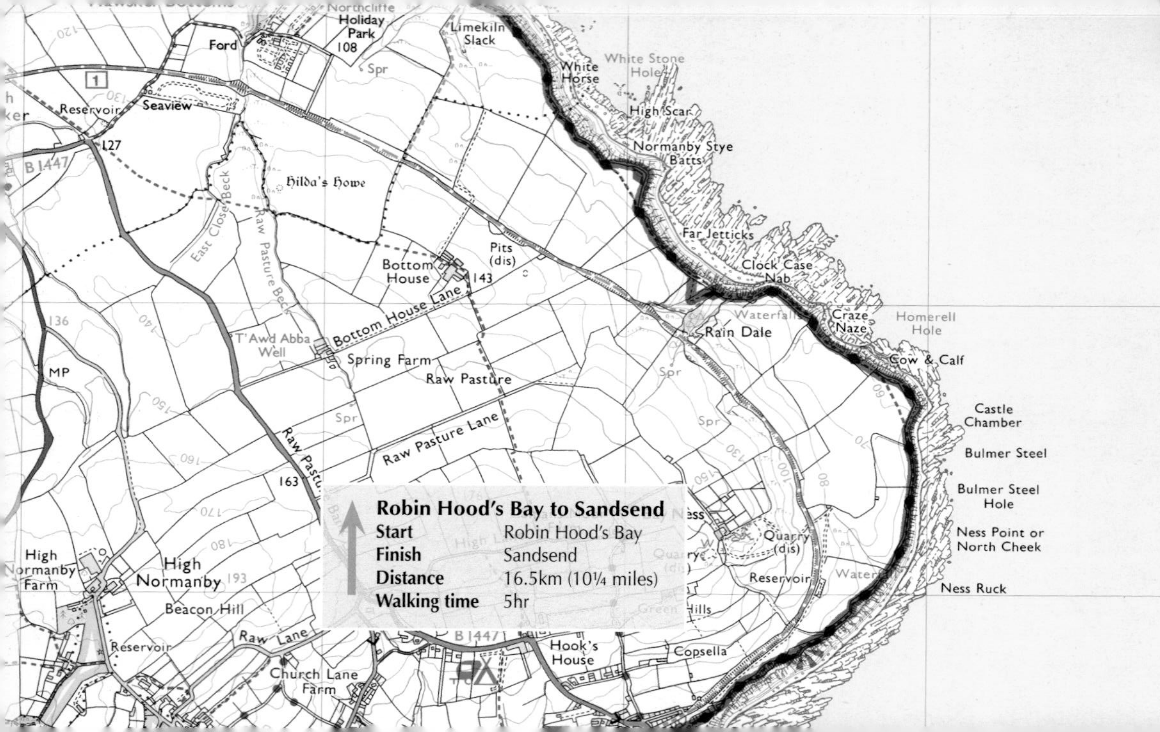

Robin Hood's Bay to Sandsend

Start	Robin Hood's Bay
Finish	Sandsend
Distance	16.5km (10¼ miles)
Walking time	5hr

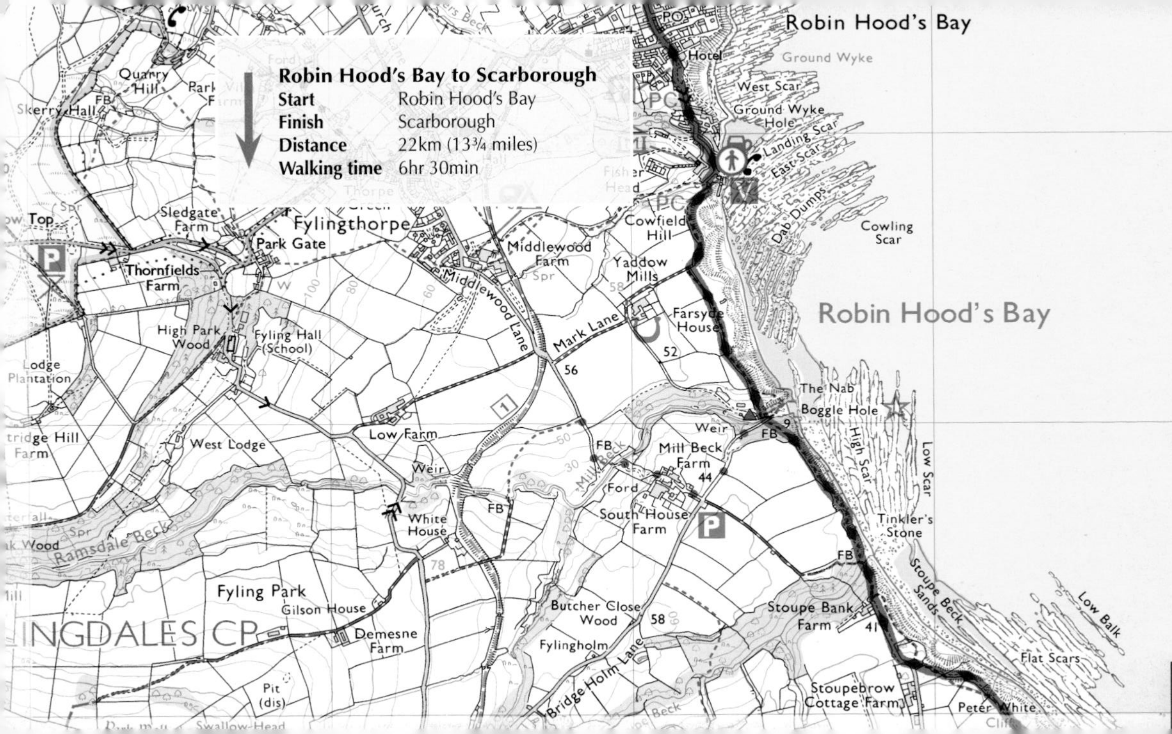
Robin Hood's Bay to Scarborough
Start Robin Hood's Bay
Finish Scarborough
Distance 22km (13¾ miles)
Walking time 6hr 30min
Robin Hood's Bay
Robin Hood's Bay
Ground Wyke
West Scar
Ground Wyke Hole
Landing Scar
East Scar
Dab Dumps
Cowling Scar
Hotel
Cowfield Hill
Yaddow Mills
Farsyde House
The Nab
Boggle Hole
High Scar
Low Scar
Tinkler's Stone
Stoupe Beck Sands
Low Balk
Flat Scars
Peter White
Stoupebrow Cottage Farm
Stoupe Bank Farm
Mill Beck Farm
South House Farm
Weir
Ford
Mark Lane
Middlewood Farm
Middlewood Lane
Fylingthorpe
Park Gate
Fyling Hall (School)
High Park Wood
Thornfields Farm
Sledgate Farm
Quarry Hill
Skerry Hall
Lodge Plantation
Low Farm
White House
West Lodge
Ramsdale Beck
Butcher Close Wood
Fylingholm
Bridge Holm Lane
Demesne Farm
Gilson House
Fyling Park
Pit (dis)
INGDALES CP
Swallow Head

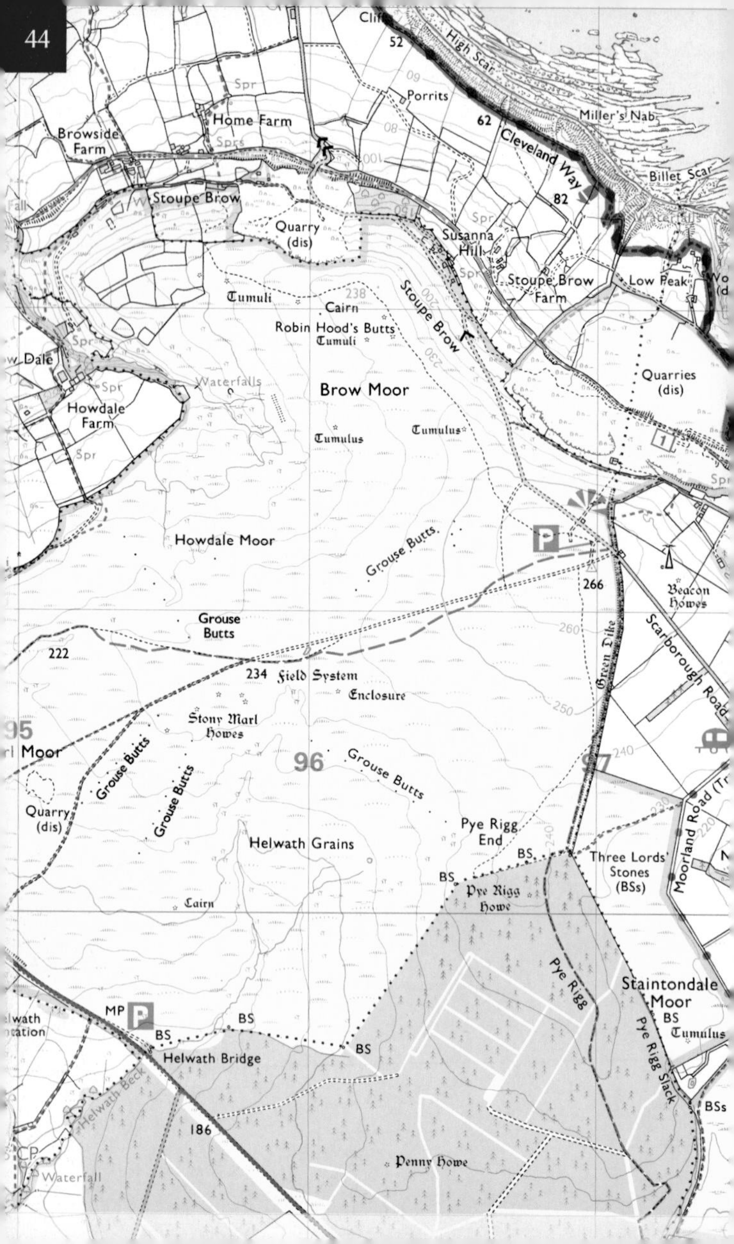
High Scar
Miller's Nab
Billet Scar
Cleveland Way
Porrits
Home Farm
Browside Farm
Stoupe Brow
Quarry (dis)
Susanna Hill
Stoupe Brow Farm
Low Peak
Tumuli
Cairn
Robin Hood's Butts
Tumuli
Stoupe Brow
Quarries (dis)
Waterfalls
Howdale Farm
Brow Moor
Tumulus
Tumulus
Howdale Moor
Grouse Butts
Beacon Howes
266
Grouse Butts
222
234
Field System
Enclosure
Green Dike
Scarborough Road
Stony Marl Howes
Grouse Butts
Grouse Butts
Grouse Butts
Quarry (dis)
Helwath Grains
Pye Rigg End
Three Lords' Stones (BSs)
Moorland Road
Pye Rigg Howe
Cairn
Pye Rigg
Staintondale Moor
Tumulus
Pye Rigg Slack
MP
Helwath Bridge
Helwath Beck
186
Penny Howe
Waterfall

Low Nook
Peak Steel
Haven
Old Peak or South Cheek
The Coomb
Raven Hall Hotel
Rocket Post
188
Blea Wyke
Blea Wyke Steel
Blea Wyke Point
Station Road
186
PC
Ravenscar
Raven Hill
Church Farm
Church Road Farm
211
Coney Well Spring
Bent Rigg Farm
Common Cliff
233
Beacon Windmill (dis)
Springfield Farm
189
Bent Rigg Lane
98
99
Bent Rigg
Wellfield Farm
Rocky Point
Waterfall
Slack
200
190
197
War Dike Gate
Tumulus
War Dike Lane
Beast Cliff
Bell Hill
180
170
Moorland House
207
Rudda Farm
STA
Sandyb
Woo
Rudda Road
Tumulus
Prospect House Farm
151
map continued
Petard Point
Waterfall
Meeting House Farm
Church

Cleveland Way
Petard Point
124
Rigg Hall Farm
East Side Farm
109
Plane Tree Cottages
98
Whitehouse Farm
72
Whitestone
Red House Farm
Herbert Hole
Mean High Water
Mean Low Water
Hayburn Wyke
Hayburn Beck
Hotel
FB
Nab End
108
97
Moor Lodge
Little Cliff
Tindall Point
Newlands
159

Iron Scar
Rodger Trod
Sycarham Farm
Salt Pans
Cloughton Wyke
Hundale Scar
Hundale Point
The Hundales
Creek Point
Long Nab
Cleveland Way
Hun Dale
Cloughton Fields Farm
Newlands Farm
Cloughton Newlands
Greystone Farm
Cober
Cober Hill
Town Farm
Cloughton
Goose Dale
FBs
PO
Ford
Quarry Banks
Caywood Plantation
The Hulleys
CLOUGHTON CP
96
95
Holm Slack
Little Moor
Little Moor Slack
A171
MS
Ripley's Bank
Spr
Sprs
112
82
66
55
97
120
100
130
140
125
115
135
60
50
40
30
70
80
90
65
75
85
45

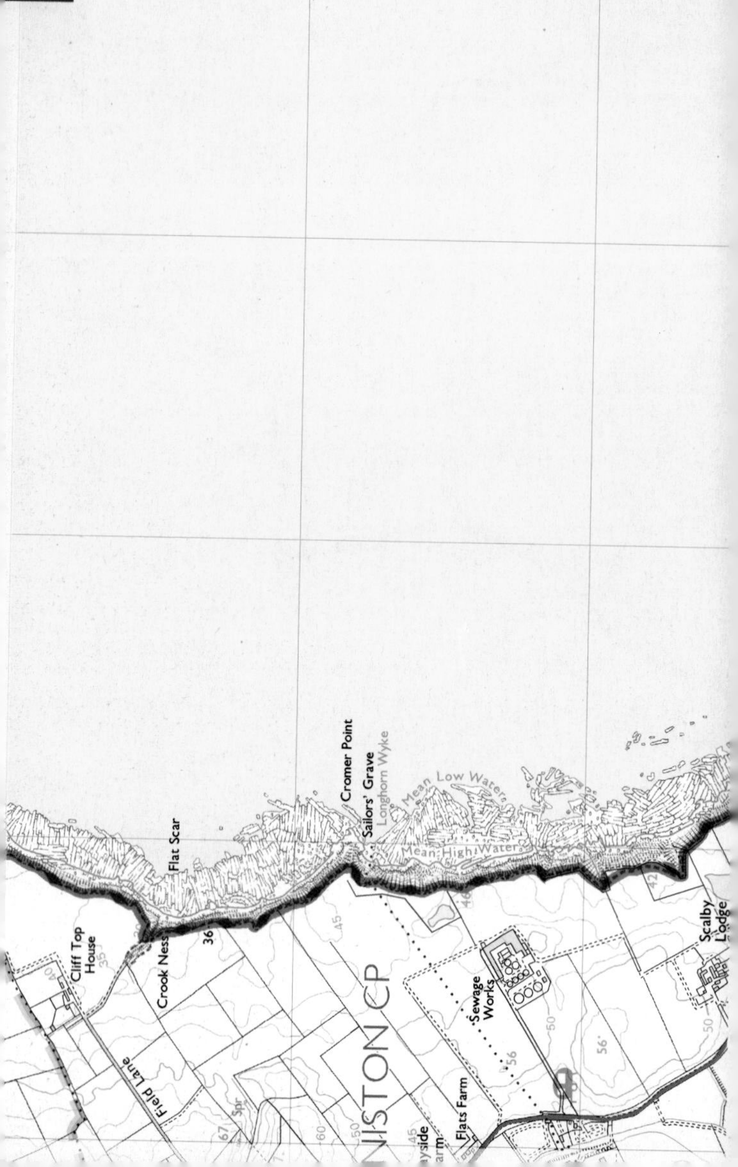
Cliff Top House
Crook Ness
Flat Scar
Cromer Point
Sailors' Grave
Longhorn Wyke
Mean Low Water
Mean High Water
NISTON CP
Sewage Works
Scalby Lodge
Field Lane
Flats Farm
Spr

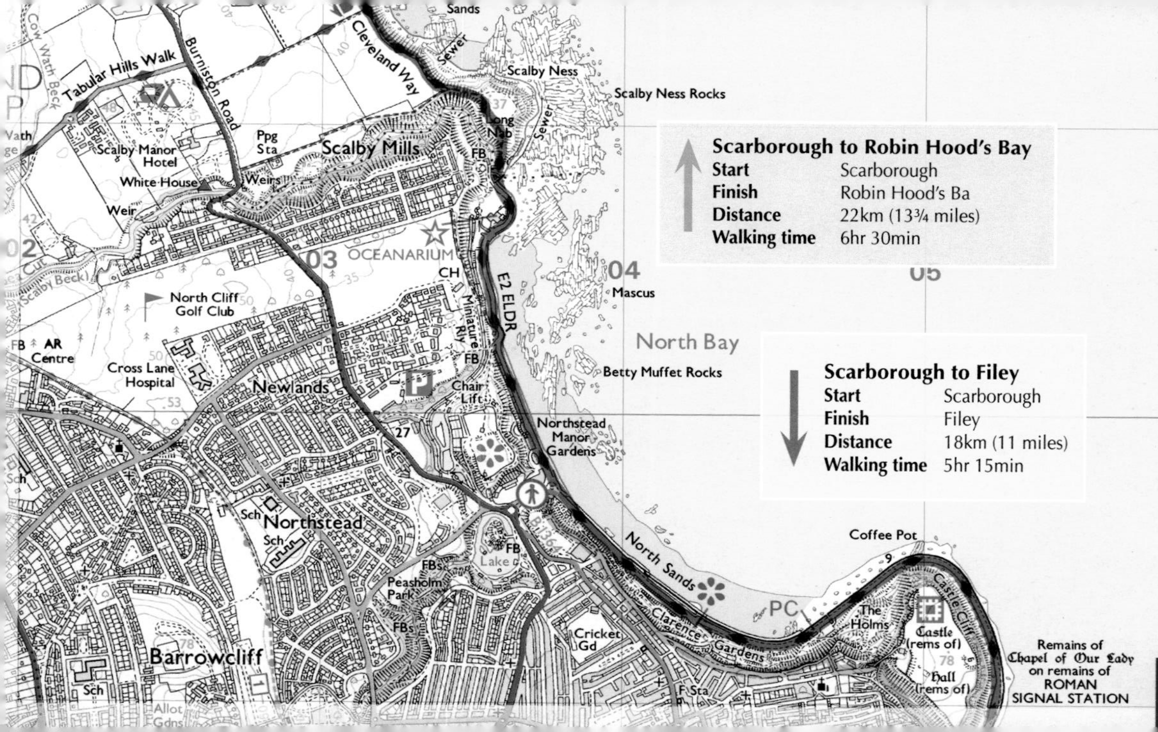

Scarborough to Robin Hood's Bay

Start	Scarborough
Finish	Robin Hood's Ba
Distance	22km (13¾ miles)
Walking time	6hr 30min

Scarborough to Filey

Start	Scarborough
Finish	Filey
Distance	18km (11 miles)
Walking time	5hr 15min

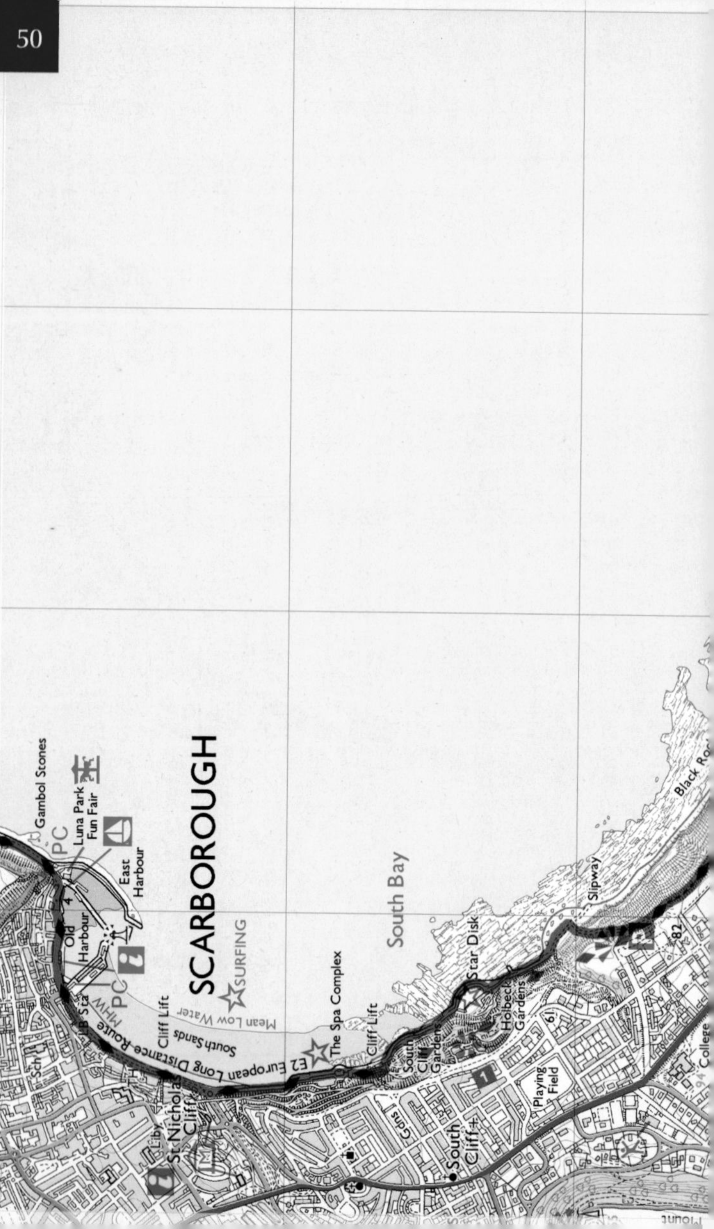
SIGNAL STATION
Gambol Stones
PC
Luna Park
Fun Fair
East
Harbour
Old
Harbour
4
LB Sta
PC
MHW
SCARBOROUGH
SURFING
Cliff Lift
Mean Low Water
South Sands
E2 European Long Distance Route
The Spa Complex
Cliff Lift
South Bay
Sch
Liby
St Nicholas
Cliff
South
Cliff
Gardens
Star Disk
Holbeck
Gardens
61
Slipway
82
Playing
Field
Gdns
South
Cliff
College
94

Red Cliff Hole
Calf Allen Rocks
Mean Low Water
Mean High Water
Cayton Bay
SURFING
Cayton Sands
Karl Stones
Ppg Sta
PC
P
48
Osgodby Point
or
Knipe Point
Johnny Flinton's Harbour
OSGODBY
Tenants' Cliff
Osgodby Hill
Cow Leys Farm
Perilous Rocks
Cornelian Bay
High Scar
Outer Lake
Inner Lake
Frank Cliff
Cayton Cliff
78
Cleveland Way
Pipe Line
Wheatcroft
Ppg Sta
74
Resr
FB
Chapel (rems of)
Osgodby
Osgodby Lane
Playing Field
Playing Fields
Schools
EASTFIELD CP
Eastfield
Deep Dale
Kit Rigg
Middle Deepdale
Knox Hill
University
A165
Scarborough South Cliff Golf Club
CH
94
113

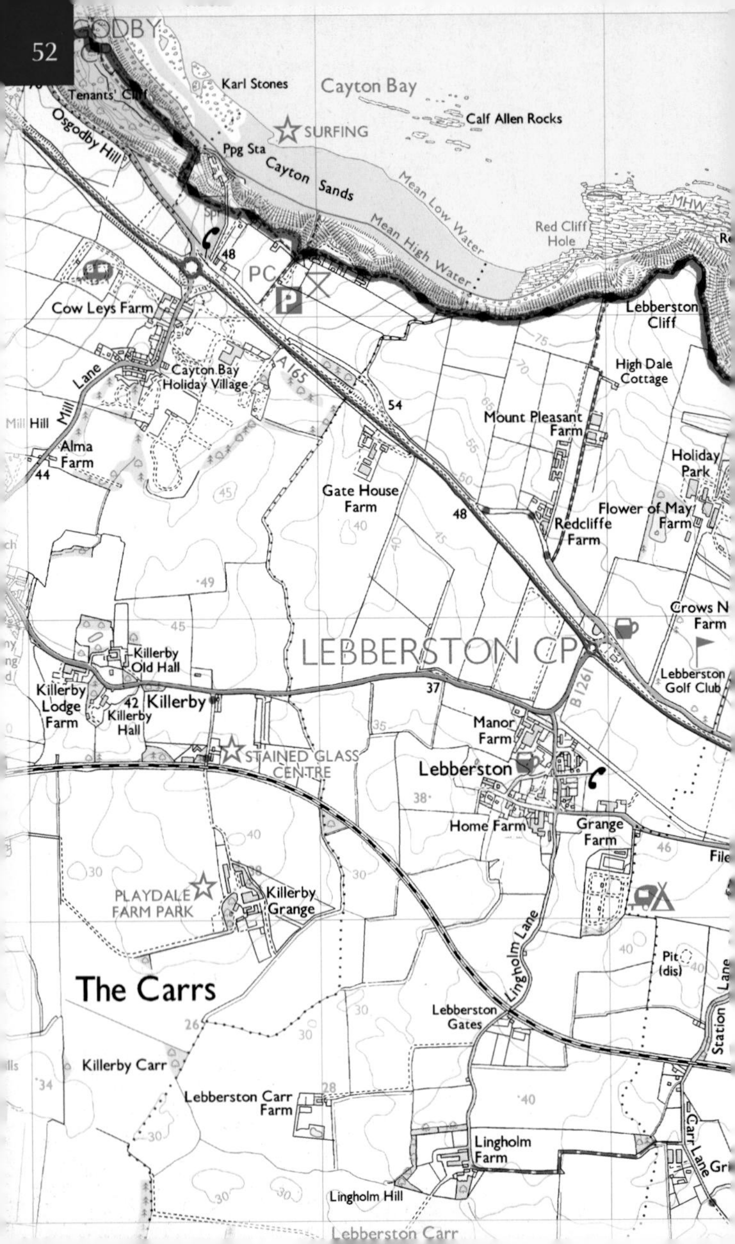
Karl Stones
Cayton Bay
Tenants' Cliff
Calf Allen Rocks
Osgodby Hill
SURFING
Ppg Sta
Cayton Sands
Mean Low Water
Mean High Water
MHW
Red Cliff Hole
48
PC
Cow Leys Farm
Lebberston Cliff
High Dale Cottage
Mill Lane
Cayton Bay Holiday Village
A165
54
Mill Hill
Mount Pleasant Farm
Alma Farm
44
Holiday Park
Gate House Farm
Flower of May Farm
48
Redcliffe Farm
Crows N Farm
LEBBERSTON CP
Killerby Old Hall
Lebberston Golf Club
B1261
37
Killerby Lodge Farm
42
Killerby
Killerby Hall
Manor Farm
STAINED GLASS CENTRE
Lebberston
Home Farm
Grange Farm
PLAYDALE FARM PARK
Killerby Grange
Lingholm Lane
Pit (dis)
The Carrs
Lebberston Gates
Station Lane
Killerby Carr
Lebberston Carr Farm
Lingholm Farm
Carr Lane
Lingholm Hill
Lebberston Carr

85
84
83
82
81
Point
ns Nab
Castle Rocks
Casty Rocks
Gristhorpe Sands
Old Horse Rocks
Old Horse
Gristhorpe Cliff
Great Dike
88
Blue Dolphin Holiday Park
90
Tumulus
85
Cunstone Nab
Cliffe House Farm
87
The Wyke
80
Cliff Farm
78
Newbiggin Cliff
Under Nine
75
epit Lane
GRISTHORPE CP
Cricket Gd
60
55
50
Rising Sun Farm
Hall
Newbiggin East Farm
Madge Hill
Newbiggin West Farm
Filey Field
Moat
Carless Farm
38
40
Gristhorpe
35
A 1039
30
29
Mill Hill
Filey Field Farm
Brookfield Farm
42
FB
Muston Cottage Farm
Crayke House Farm
35
34
40
40
Carr
30
42
30

Filey to Scarborough

Start	Filey
Finish	Scarborough
Distance	18km (11 miles)
Walking time	5hr 15min

Filey Brigg
Brigg End
14
15
1

Map data

LEGEND OF SYMBOLS USED ON ORDNANCE SURVEY 1:25,000 (EXPLORER) MAPPING

ROADS AND PATHS

Not necessarily rights of way

M1 or A6(M)	Motorway	Service Area	7 Junction Number
A 35	Dual carriageway	Service Area	T1 Toll road junction
A30	Main road		
B 3074	Secondary road		
	Narrow road with passing places		
	Road under construction		
	Road generally more than 4 m wide		
	Road generally less than 4 m wide		
	Other road, drive or track, fenced and unfenced		
	Gradient: steeper than 20% (1 in 5); 14% (1 in 7) to 20% (1 in 5)		
Ferry	Ferry; Ferry P – passenger only		
	Path		

RAILWAYS

- Multiple track } standard gauge
- Single track } standard gauge
- Narrow gauge or Light rapid transit system (LRTS) and station
- Road over; road under; level crossing
- Cutting; tunnel; embankment
- Station, open to passengers; siding

PUBLIC RIGHTS OF WAY

- Footpath
- Bridleway
- Byway open to all traffic
- Restricted byway

The representation on this map of any other road, track or path is no evidence of the existence of a right of way

ARCHAEOLOGICAL AND HISTORICAL INFORMATION

✣	Site of antiquity	VILLA	Roman	⋆	Visible earthwork
⚔ 1066	Site of battle (with date)	Castle	Non-Roman		

Information provided by English Heritage for England and the Royal Commissions on the Ancient and Historical Monuments for Scotland and Wales

OTHER PUBLIC ACCESS

• • •	Other routes with public access	The exact nature of the rights on these routes and the existence of any restrictions may be checked with the local highway authority. Alignments are based on the best information available
◆ ◆ ◆	Recreational route	
◆ ◆ ◆	🚶 National Trail (✦) Long Distance Route	
- - - - - -	Permissive footpath	Footpaths and bridleways along which landowners have permitted public use but which are not rights of way. The agreement may be withdrawn
— — — —	Permissive bridleway	
• • •	Traffic-free cycle route	
1 1	National cycle network route number – traffic free; on road	

ACCESS LAND

 Firing and test ranges in the area. Danger! Observe warning notices

 Access permitted within managed controls, for example, local byelaws. Visit **www.access.mod.uk** for information

England and Wales

 Access land boundary and tint

Access land in wooded area

 Access information point

Portrayal of access land on this map is intended as a guide to land which is normally available for access on foot, for example access land created under the Countryside and Rights of Way Act 2000, and land managed by the National Trust, Forestry Commission and Woodland Trust. Access for other activities may also exist. Some restrictions will apply; some land will be excluded from open access rights. The depiction of rights of access does not imply or express any warranty as to its accuracy or completeness. Observe local signs and follow the Countryside Code. Visit **www.countrysideaccess.gov.uk** for up-to-date information

BOUNDARIES

— + — +	National
— · — · —	County (England)
— — — —	Unitary Authority (UA), Metropolitan District (Met Dist), London Borough (LB) or District (Scotland & Wales are solely Unitary Authorities)
· · · · · · · ·	Civil Parish (CP) (England) or Community (C) (Wales)
▬▬ ▬▬	National Park boundary

VEGETATION

Limits of vegetation are defined by positioning of symbols

Coniferous trees
Non-coniferous trees
Coppice
Orchard
Scrub
Bracken, heath or rough grassland
Marsh, reeds or saltings

HEIGHTS AND NATURAL FEATURES

52 · Ground survey height
284 · Air survey height

Surface heights are to the nearest metre above mean sea level. Where two heights are shown, the first height is to the base of the triangulation pillar and the second (in brackets) to the highest natural point of the hill

HEIGHTS AND NATURAL FEATURES (continued)

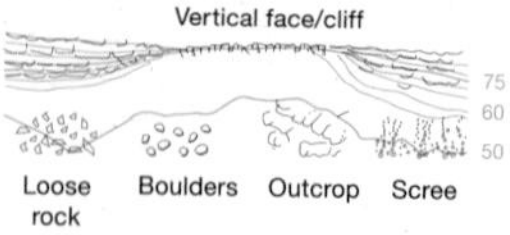

Contours are at 5 or 10 metre vertical intervals

- Water
- Mud
- Sand; sand and shingle

SELECTED TOURIST AND LEISURE INFORMATION

- Building of historic interest
- Cadw
- Heritage centre
- Camp site
- Caravan site
- Camping and caravan site
- Castle / fort
- Cathedral / Abbey
- Craft centre
- Country park
- Cycle trail
- Mountain bike trail
- Cycle hire
- English Heritage
- Fishing
- Forestry Commission Visitor centre
- Garden / arboretum
- Golf course or links
- Historic Scotland
- Information centre, all year
- Information centre, seasonal
- Horse riding
- Museum
- National Park Visitor Centre (park logo) e.g. Yorkshire Dales
- Nature reserve
- National Trust
- Other tourist feature
- Parking
- Park and ride, all year
- Park and ride, seasonal
- Picnic site
- Preserved railway
- PC Public Convenience
- Public house/s
- Recreation / leisure / sports centre
- Roman site (Hadrian's Wall only)
- Slipway
- Telephone, emergency
- Telephone, public
- Telephone, roadside assistance
- Theme / pleasure park
- Viewpoint
- Visitor centre
- Walks / trails
- World Heritage site / area
- Water activites
- Boat trips
- Boat hire

(For complete legend and symbols, see any OS Explorer map).

THE CLEVELAND WAY

This map booklet accompanies Paddy Dillon's guidebook to walking the Cleveland Way, described from Helmsley to Filey. The guidebook also describes the Tabular Hills Walk which closes the loop of the Cleveland Way walk, and the Yorkshire Wolds Way which links end to end with the Cleveland Way on the coast. The guidebook features annotated 1:50,000 mapping alongside detailed route descriptions and planning information.

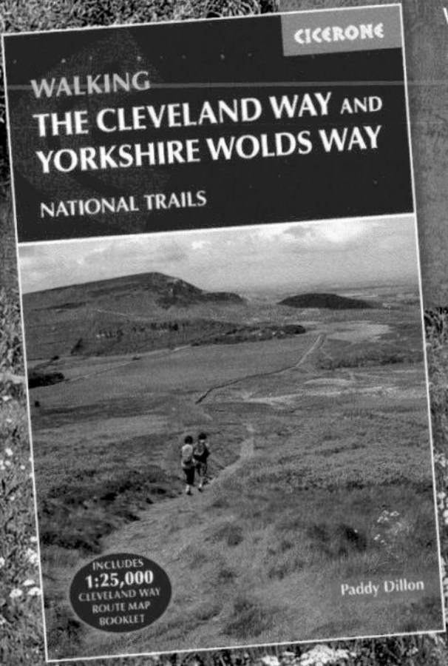

The Sea Cut leads far inland from Scalby Mills to Mowthorpe Bridge (Day 1 of the Tabular Hills Walk)

OTHER CICERONE TRAIL GUIDES

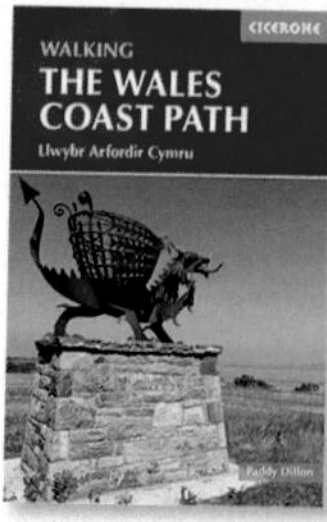

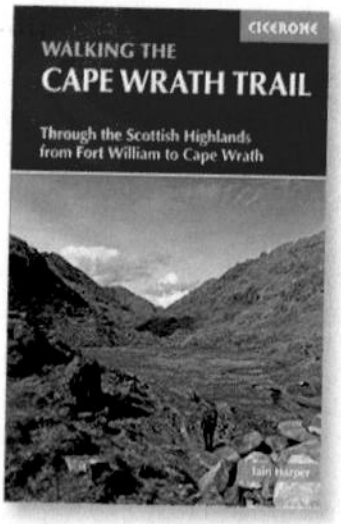

Cicerone National Trails Guides

The South West Coast Path
The South Downs Way
The North Downs Way
The Ridgeway National Trail
The Thames Path
The Cotswold Way
The Peddars Way and
Norfolk Coast Path
The Cleveland Way and
the Yorkshire Wolds Way
Cycling the Pennine Bridleway
The Pennine Way
Hadrian's Wall Path
The Pembrokeshire Coast Path
Offa's Dyke Path
Glyndŵr's Way

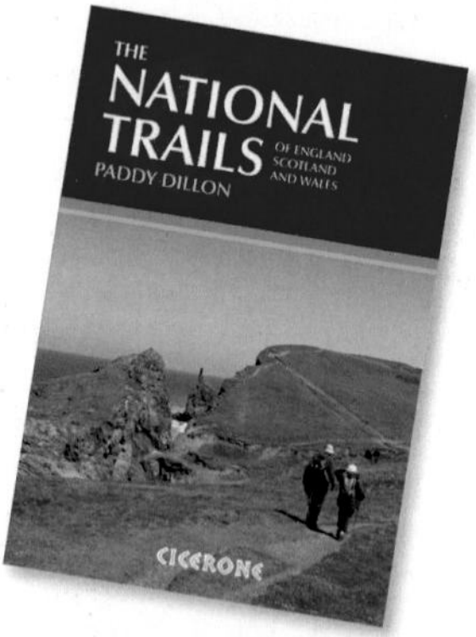

Scotland's Great Trails

The Southern Upland Way
The Speyside Way
The West Highland Way
The Great Glen Way

Visit our website for a full
list of Cicerone Trail Guides
www.cicerone.co.uk

CICERONE

LISTING OF CICERONE GUIDES

BRITISH ISLES CHALLENGES, COLLECTIONS AND ACTIVITIES

The Book of the Bivvy
The Book of the Bothy
The End to End Trail
The Mountains of England and Wales: 1&2
The National Trails
The Relative Hills of Britain
The Ridges of England, Wales and Ireland
The UK Trailwalker's Handbook
The UK's County Tops
Three Peaks, Ten Tors

UK CYCLING

20 Classic Sportive Rides
South West England
South East England
Border Country Cycle Routes
Cycling in the Cotswolds
Cycling in the Hebrides
Cycling in the Peak District
Cycling in the Yorkshire Dales
Cycling the Pennine Bridleway
Mountain Biking in the Lake District
Mountain Biking in the Yorkshire Dales
Mountain Biking on the North Downs
Mountain Biking on the South Downs
The C2C Cycle Route
The End to End Cycle Route
The Lancashire Cycleway

UK BACKPACKING

Backpacker's Britain
Northern Scotland

SCOTLAND

Ben Nevis and Glen Coe
Great Mountain Days in Scotland
Not the West Highland Way
Scotland's Best Small Mountains
Scotland's Far West
Scotland's Mountain Ridges
Scrambles in Lochaber
The Ayrshire and Arran Coastal Paths
The Border Country
The Cape Wrath Trail
The Great Glen Way
The Hebrides
The Isle of Mull
The Isle of Skye
The Pentland Hills
The Skye Trail
The Southern Upland Way
The Speyside Way
The West Highland Way
Walking Highland Perthshire
Walking in Scotland's Far North
Walking in the Angus Glens
Walking in the Cairngorms
Walking in the Ochils, Campsie Fells and Lomond Hills
Walking in the Southern Uplands
Walking in Torridon
Walking Loch Lomond and the Trossachs
Walking on Arran
Walking on Harris and Lewis
Walking on Jura, Islay and Colonsay
Walking on Rum and the Small Isles
Walking on the Isle of Arran
Walking on the Orkney and Shetland Isles
Walking on Uist and Barra
Walking the Corbetts
1 South of the Great Glen
2 North of the Great Glen
Walking the Galloway Hills
Walking the Munros
1 Southern, Central and Western Highlands
2 Northern Highlands and the Cairngorms
Winter Climbs Ben Nevis and Glen Coe
Winter Climbs in the Cairngorms
World Mountain Ranges: Scotland

NORTHERN ENGLAND TRAILS

A Northern Coast to Coast Walk
Hadrian's Wall Path
The Dales Way
The Pennine Way

NORTH EAST ENGLAND, YORKSHIRE DALES AND PENNINES

Great Mountain Days in the Pennines
Historic Walks in North Yorkshire
South Pennine Walks
St Oswald's Way and St Cuthbert's Way
The North York Moors
The Reivers Way
The Teesdale Way
The Yorkshire Dales
North and East
South and West
Walking in County Durham
Walking in Northumberland
Walking in the North Pennines
Walks in Dales Country
Walks in the Yorkshire Dales

NORTH WEST ENGLAND AND THE ISLE OF MAN

Historic Walks in Cheshire
Isle of Man Coastal Path
The Lune Valley and Howgills
The Ribble Way
Walking in Cumbria's Eden Valley
Walking in Lancashire
Walking in the Forest of Bowland and Pendle
Walking on the Isle of Man
Walking on the West Pennine Moors
Walks in Lancashire Witch Country
Walks in Ribble Country
Walks in Silverdale and Arnside
Walks in the Forest of Bowland

LAKE DISTRICT

Coniston Copper Mines
Great Mountain Days in the Lake District
Lake District Winter Climbs
Lake District: High Level and Fell Walks
Lake District: Low Level and Lake Walks
Lakeland Fellranger
The Central Fells
The Far-Eastern Fells
The Mid-Western Fells
The Near Eastern Fells
The Northern Fells
The North-Western Fells
The Southern Fells
The Western Fells
Rocky Rambler's Wild Walks

Scrambles in the Lake District North & South
Short Walks in Lakeland
1 South Lakeland
2 North Lakeland
3 West Lakeland
The Cumbria Way

DERBYSHIRE, PEAK DISTRICT AND MIDLANDS

High Peak Walks
Scrambles in the Dark Peak
The Star Family Walks
Walking in Derbyshire
White Peak Walks
The Northern Dales
The Southern Dales

SOUTHERN ENGLAND

Suffolk Coast & Heaths Walks
The Great Stones Way
The Lea Valley Walk
The North Downs Way
The Peddars Way and Norfolk Coast Path
The Ridgeway National Trail
The South Downs Way
The South West Coast Path
The Thames Path
The Two Moors Way
Walking in Cornwall
Walking in Essex
Walking in Kent
Walking in Norfolk
Walking in Sussex
Walking in the Chilterns
Walking in the Cotswolds
Walking in the Isles of Scilly
Walking in the New Forest
Walking in the North Wessex Downs
Walking in the Thames Valley
Walking on Dartmoor
Walking on Guernsey
Walking on Jersey
Walking on the Isle of Wight
Walking the Jurassic Coast
Walks in the South Downs National Park

WALES AND WELSH BORDERS

Glyndwr's Way
Great Mountain Days in Snowdonia
Hillwalking in Snowdonia
Hillwalking in Wales: 1&2
Offa's Dyke Path
Ridges of Snowdonia
Scrambles in Snowdonia
The Ascent of Snowdon
The Ceredigion and Snowdonia Coast Paths
Lleyn Peninsula Coastal Path
Pembrokeshire Coastal Path
The Severn Way
The Shropshire Hills
The Wales Coast Path
The Wye Valley Walk
Walking in Carmarthenshire
Walking in Pembrokeshire
Walking in the Forest of Dean
Walking in the South Wales Valleys
Walking in the Wye Valley
Walking on the Brecon Beacons
Walking on the Gower
Welsh Winter Climbs

INTERNATIONAL CHALLENGES, COLLECTIONS AND ACTIVITIES

Canyoning
Canyoning in the Alps
Europe's High Points
The Via Francigena: 1&2

EUROPEAN CYCLING

Cycle Touring in France
Cycle Touring in Ireland
Cycle Touring in Spain
Cycle Touring in Switzerland
Cycling in the French Alps
Cycling the Canal du Midi
Cycling the River Loire
The Danube Cycleway: 1&2
The Grand Traverse of the Massif Central
The Moselle Cycle Route
The Rhine Cycle Route
The Way of St James

AFRICA

Climbing in the Moroccan Anti-Atlas
Kilimanjaro
Mountaineering in the Moroccan High Atlas
The High Atlas
Trekking in the Atlas Mountains
Walking in the Drakensberg

ALPS – CROSS-BORDER ROUTES

100 Hut Walks in the Alps
Across the Eastern Alps: E5
Alpine Points of View
Alpine Ski Mountaineering
1 Western Alps
2 Central and Eastern Alps
Chamonix to Zermatt
The Tour of the Bernina
Tour of Mont Blanc
Tour of Monte Rosa
Tour of the Matterhorn
Trekking in the Alps
Trekking in the Silvretta and Rätikon Alps
Walking in the Alps
Walks and Treks in the Maritime Alps

PYRENEES AND FRANCE/ SPAIN CROSS-BORDER ROUTES

The GR10 Trail
The GR11 Trail – La Senda
The Mountains of Andorra
The Pyrenean Haute Route
The Pyrenees
The Way of St James: France & Spain
Walks and Climbs in the Pyrenees

AUSTRIA

The Adlerweg
Trekking in Austria's Hohe Tauern
Trekking in the Stubai Alps
Trekking in the Zillertal Alps
Walking in Austria

BELGIUM AND LUXEMBOURG

Walking in the Ardennes

EASTERN EUROPE

The High Tatras
The Mountains of Romania
Walking in Bulgaria's National Parks
Walking in Hungary

FRANCE

Chamonix Mountain Adventures
Ecrins National Park
Mont Blanc Walks
Mountain Adventures in the Maurienne

The Cathar Way
The GR20 Corsica
The GR5 Trail
The Robert Louis Stevenson Trail
Tour of the Oisans: The GR54
Tour of the Queyras
Tour of the Vanoise
Vanoise Ski Touring
Via Ferratas of the French Alps
Walking in Corsica
Walking in Provence – East
Walking in Provence – West
Walking in the Auvergne
Walking in the Cevennes
Walking in the Dordogne
Walking in the Haute Savoie – North & South
Walks in the Cathar Region

GERMANY

Hiking and Biking in the Black Forest
Walking in the Bavarian Alps

HIMALAYA

Annapurna
Bhutan
Everest
The Mount Kailash Trek
Trekking in Ladakh
Trekking in the Himalaya

ICELAND & GREENLAND

Trekking in Greenland
Walking and Trekking in Iceland

IRELAND

The Irish Coast to Coast Walk
The Mountains of Ireland

ITALY

Gran Paradiso
Sibillini National Park
Shorter Walks in the Dolomites
The Way of St Francis
Through the Italian Alps
Trekking in the Apennines
Trekking in the Dolomites
Via Ferratas of the Italian Dolomites: 1&2
Walking in Abruzzo
Walking in Italy's Stelvio National Park
Walking in Sardinia
Walking in Sicily
Walking in the Central Italian Alps
Walking in the Dolomites
Walking in Tuscany
Walking in Umbria
Walking on the Amalfi Coast
Walking the Italian Lakes

MEDITERRANEAN

Jordan – Walks, Treks, Caves, Climbs and Canyons
The High Mountains of Crete
The Mountains of Greece
Treks and Climbs in Wadi Rum
Walking and Trekking on Corfu
Walking on Malta
Western Crete

NORTH AMERICA

British Columbia
The Grand Canyon
The John Muir Trail
The Pacific Crest Trail

SOUTH AMERICA

Aconcagua and the Southern Andes
Hiking and Biking Peru's Inca Trails
Torres del Paine

SCANDINAVIA

Walking in Norway

SLOVENIA, CROATIA AND MONTENEGRO

The Islands of Croatia
The Julian Alps of Slovenia
The Mountains of Montenegro
Trekking in Slovenia
Walking in Croatia
Walking in Slovenia: The Karavanke

SPAIN AND PORTUGAL

Mountain Walking in Southern Catalunya
Spain's Sendero Histórico: The GR1
The Mountains of Nerja
The Northern Caminos
Trekking through Mallorca
Walking in Andalucia
Walking in Madeira
Walking in Mallorca
Walking in Menorca
Walking in the Algarve
Walking in the Cordillera Cantabrica
Walking in the Sierra Nevada
Walking on Gran Canaria
Walking on La Gomera and El Hierro
Walking on La Palma
Walking on Lanzarote and Fuerteventura
Walking on Tenerife
Walking the GR7 in Andalucia
Walks and Climbs in the Picos de Europa

SWITZERLAND

Alpine Pass Route
The Swiss Alps
Tour of the Jungfrau Region
Walking in the Bernese Oberland
Walking in the Valais
Walks in the Engadine

TECHNIQUES

Geocaching in the UK
Indoor Climbing
Lightweight Camping
Map and Compass
Mountain Weather
Outdoor Photography
Polar Exploration
Rock Climbing
Sport Climbing
The Hillwalker's Manual

MINI GUIDES

Alpine Flowers
Avalanche!
Navigating with a GPS
Navigation
Pocket First Aid and Wilderness Medicine
Snow

MOUNTAIN LITERATURE

8000 metres
A Walk in the Clouds
Abode of the Gods
Unjustifiable Risk?

For full information on all our guides, books and eBooks, visit our website: **www.cicerone.co.uk**.

Walking – Trekking – Mountaineering – Climbing – Cycling

Over 40 years, Cicerone have built up an outstanding collection of over 300 guides, inspiring all sorts of amazing adventures.

Every guide comes from extensive exploration and research by our expert authors, all with a passion for their subjects. They are frequently praised, endorsed and used by clubs, instructors and outdoor organisations.

All our titles can now be bought as **e-books**, **ePubs** and **Kindle** files and we also have an online magazine – **Cicerone Extra** – with features to help cyclists, climbers, walkers and trekkers choose their next adventure, at home or abroad.

Our website shows any **new information** we've had in since a book was published. Please do let us know if you find anything has changed, so that we can publish the latest details. On our **website** you'll also find great ideas and lots of detailed information about what's inside every guide and you can buy **individual routes** from many of them online.

It's easy to keep in touch with what's going on at Cicerone by getting our monthly **free e-newsletter**, which is full of offers, competitions, up-to-date information and topical articles. You can subscribe on our home page and also follow us on **Facebook** and **Twitter** or dip into our **blog**.

Cicerone – the very best guides for exploring the world.

CICERONE

2 Police Square Milnthorpe Cumbria LA7 7PY
Tel: 015395 62069 info@cicerone.co.uk
www.cicerone.co.uk and **www.cicerone-extra.com**